TABLE OF CONTENTS

DAY TRADING

DAY TRADING

Quickstart Guide for Beginners with Powerful Strategies to Trade Options, Stocks, Forex, Futures, Crypto, and ETFs to Generate a Continuous Cash Flow

MARK SWING

>> INTRODUCTION <<

Congratulations on your purchase of *Day Trading: Quickstart Guide for Beginners with Powerful Strategies to Trade Options, Stocks, Forex, Futures, Crypto, and ETFs to Generate a Continuous Cash Flow*, and thank you for doing so. This is a book that I have written in a series of six. My objective is to transform any beginner investor into a successful trader in all types of financial trading, real estate, or dividend stocks by guiding them on how to make their first steps and get into the required momentum. To that effect, I have published six books, and the one you are about to read is number three in the series. In case you enjoy reading this one, which I am sure you will, feel free to download the others, as they will be just as engaging and informative. I will list them at the end of your read, together with the links where you can download them.

Now, the trading of financial assets has been growing tremendously this decade due to more exposure of people to the art. This is the decade when small-scale traders and individuals have been enabled to trade. In the past, trading was reserved for the big boys and institutions who could afford the hefty requirements, such as capital running into the millions of dollars. Today, thanks to brokers and the use of something called leverage, which we are going to discuss later, anybody can trade with only a smartphone, computer, and a few dollars.

As the industry grows, so has false information. One of the biggest lies being thrown at innocent would-be traders is that it is an easy art. Assuming that you have not traded before, you might have already come across an online ad telling you, "Trading is easy. Just do ABC, and you will be making millions in a month!" If you have ever been curious enough to follow through with such an advert to the end, their objective is usually, "Sign up with us to start your journey into the millionaires' club." It is all pure marketing fluff.

Make no mistake; trading can be made simple, but it is not easy! As much as there are tons of websites and intruding ads that try to make you believe this misconception, any established trader like me will advise you otherwise. Typically, ads will make you believe that after reading a few books or paying for some over-promising online courses, you will automatically transform into a successful professional trader.

WRONG!

To be on the safe side, perceive any form of trading like any other profession you know. You can neither become an engineer by skimming through 200 pages of an expensive book sold on Amazon nor can you qualify to be a doctor in a week, no matter how intense your training is. In the same way, trading of any kind requires serious education before anyone can put their money on the line and start reaping profits from it. Trading, when properly done, can earn you more money than some of the best careers that you know. Ask yourself, then, how you can make more money than someone who has studied for years, yet all you did was to enroll in a 2-month course or buy a magical trading system for a couple of dollars?

To cut the long story short, congratulations for thinking differently. The reason you have decided to purchase this quick-start guide to day trading is that you understand the seriousness that trading requires. Fortunately for you, by the end of your reading, you will understand all the necessary concepts to get you started on the journey of becoming a profitable trader. That is exactly what this book was created to do. However, keep in mind that reading it will not make you successful instantaneously. Rather, it will get you started in the long journey toward understanding day trading, and, with time, you will become the successful trader that everyone dreams of becoming.

That said, here is an overview of what the chapters inside the book will look like:

- Chapter 1 will kick-start your journey to successful trading by elaborating on the meaning of online trading. In addition to the definition, we shall see the different types of online trading that exist and how to settle for the best ones.

- In Chapter 2, we are going to look at one of the markets that we shall base most of our strategies on— the forex market. This is the biggest market in the world, and, by using it as our basis for this book, we can apply the same concepts in the other markets. It is important to understand what a market entails, how it works, and the role that we play in it for us to generate consistent profits.

- Chapter 3 will highlight the four styles used in trading. These styles determine how much time a trader uses them on their platforms. This is an important chapter in which it tells us why we should opt for day trading in making a living as opposed to the other three.

- Chapter 4 will outline the basic tools that a person needs in order to start trading effectively.

- Chapter 5 contains the basic and most important words and phrases used in the online trading industry. By understanding these words, the learning experience becomes simplified and more enjoyable.

- In Chapter 6, we shall discuss some of the most common trading platforms used in online trading. In addition, we are going to look at the MT5, which we shall use for our study, in terms of installation and some types of charts found in it.

- Chapter 7 will present yet another controversial debate that begs the question, "Which one between fundamental and technical market analysis is better?" It will explain the two approaches in detail and explain why we shall choose one of them for our day trading guide.

- In chapter 8, we are going to get started with the most interesting and important approach to analyze the charts and know whether to sell or buy an instrument. We shall study the anatomy of candlesticks and what they mean. In addition, the chapter will reveal the basic but very profitable candlestick patterns used in day trading.

- Chapter 9 will talk about another crucial concept of trading known as support and resistance. These are important areas that every trader needs to be familiar with as they help them in making decisions about the management of their trades.

- Chapter 10 is about chart indicators. Unlike the two concepts discussed in chapters 8 and 9 that depend on the trader's skill, chapter 10 will introduce some automated analytic tools. These tools will help the trader to spot important information that can add to the accuracy of their signals.

- In chapter 11, we shall introduce another magical concept, which helps traders in predicting the future of the market, known as Elliot Waves. This approach is used by the best traders in the world. However, to some junior traders, it appears like a tough concept to grasp. In this guide, Elliot Waves have been laid out in simple terms so the reader can understand them and use them in their analysis with ease and accuracy.

- Chapter 12 introduces yet another popular day trading pattern that can be used in any type of market. It is similar to the Elliot Waves but has fewer waves and requires the use of an additional tool known as Fibonacci for proper analysis.

- The second-last chapter, Chapter 13, will discuss risk management. These are the proven ways that a practicing trader can minimize their losses and boost their profits in the high-risk environment of trading.

- Finally, our last chapter will discuss the final tool that a trader needs: a trading plan. This is the one tool that brings the trader life and keeps it in perfect order.

There are plenty of books on this subject on the market, so thanks again for choosing this one. Every effort was made to ensure it is full of as much useful information as possible. Please enjoy!

IMPORTANT!

Please note that day trading, like any other form of trading, is a high-risk venture. The investment or capital that you use is in trading is always at a risk of loss. Second, trading leveraged financial instruments might not be favorable for everyone. Therefore, even as you venture into online trading, make sure you have implemented the risk-managing fundamentals recommended in this book. Finally, only risk the money that you are comfortable losing.

CHAPTER 1
WHAT IS ONLINE TRADING?

Well, we are already getting started with our day trading guide. In this chapter, we are going to define the phrase "day trading" so that everyone, especially those who have never come across trading, can grasp what trading entails. As promised, this book will start you off in the context of day trading from the lowest point possible and let you go when you can successfully trade any financial asset and make profits. As such, in case you are a seasoned trader who is only interested in the day trading strategies, you might consider skipping a few chapters ahead. However, I would recommend that you skim through the earlier chapters as you might pick a tip or two that would enhance your trading experience.

DEFINITION OF ONLINE TRADING

In the simplest terms, trading is something that we do every day, although we might not refer to it that way. Whenever you exchange something in return for another, you have executed a trade. For example, when it is hot, you get some money and buy yourself some ice cream to cool yourself down. In that scenario, you have exchanged your money in return for the ice cream. The vendor, too, has given you the ice cream in exchange for your money. So, in short, we can refer to trading as the purchase and/or selling of services and goods with compensation paid to a seller by a buyer.

The same concept applies to the online trading of securities. You may get confused by this word. A "security" is any tradable financial asset. There are three categories of securities:

- Equity securities such as stocks

- Debt securities such as banknotes, cryptocurrency, and bonds

- Derivates such as options and futures

You will get to understand them better as we go along. Everything that we are going to trade and discuss falls under one of the above categories.

Trading any financial asset follows the same concept as purchasing ice cream; only this time, no physical goods or services are involved. Let us take stocks, for example. If Facebook is selling a single stock at $180, it means anyone who can afford that money can own a piece of the company. If the company's overall worth grows, so will the value of its stocks. So, if someone had bought the stock for $180 and it appreciated to $185, then they can sell the stock and make a profit of $5 for each stock they held. Remember that all this happened without them contacting or even going to Facebook. Do you get it now?

From the above explanation, we can now define online trading as the act of buying and selling financial assets (or products) over the internet. Traders, both buyers and sellers, need an online platform that brings them together and enables their exchange to happen. In online trading, financial instruments like stocks, cryptocurrency, international currencies, futures, options, and Exchange-Traded-Funds (ETFs) are involved. The internet acts as the channel through which buyers and sellers meet. The marketplace is created by intermediary parties known as "brokers." These are the firms that create trading platforms on the web and enable the exchange between the two parties to happen.

In the days before the internet was born, investors had to visit their brokers physically or make calls to them. The brokers would provide the investors with information, such as the trading time and the price of the requested financial instruments. After this, the investor would decide whether to purchase the instruments or not. If they wanted to buy them, they would tell the brokers to place the orders for them. Once they had made some profits, it was the broker who would get the money and pay the traders physically. If the traders made losses, they would give the money to the brokers to deposit it for them, so they could trade again in the future. This is how lengthy and tedious traditional trading was before the internet age.

Today, trading has become a self-service. An investor can do everything from the comfort of their home. With a computer, anyone can access market information, deposit their money, execute trades, and withdraw their profits without involving any third parties. However, a broker is necessary since they provide the platforms required for these processes.

TYPES OF TRADING MARKETS

As you might have noticed, trading is a very wide industry. By the time you finally decide to start day trading, you must have decided on the type of market or markets that you will be trading. This is because each market behaves differently and might have unique requirements. All the same, the methods of trading that you will learn can be applied in any market that you choose. The main differences between different markets lie in the type of asset that is being traded, the volume of the assets (size of the market), volatility (the rate of price changes), and the amount of investment capital required.

Let us look at some of the major markets that you can choose from.

1. The Forex Market

The forex market is the biggest financial market in the world today. The name "forex" is coined from the words "Foreign" and "Exchange." In essence, when trading forex, you are simply making money by exchanging one currency for another. For instance, you can use US Dollars to purchased Japanese Yen (JPY). When the value of the USD increases or that of the JPY decreases, you can make profits from that exchange. We are going to delve deeper into the forex market as it will form the basis of our strategies since it is the most traded market in the world, and the strategies applied in trading currencies can be used in any other market.

2. The Stock Market

The stock market is the oldest financial market that has been in existence decades before the forex market was born. Today, it is still very popular despite trailing the forex market by far. When trading the stock market, you are simply buying and selling the shares of a particular company such as Google, Amazon, Shell, Facebook, Bing, and so on. In addition to the shares, stock trading also allows the trading of indices like:

- **DAX 30:** This is a collection of the top 30 companies in Germany that are listed on the Frankfurt Stock Exchange.

- **FTSE 100:** This is a collection of the top 100 companies listed on the London Stock Exchange.

- **S&P 500:** This is a collection of the top 500 of the most traded stocks (shares) in the United States.

- **Dow Jones:** This is a collection of 30 of the biggest and most influential companies in the United States.

- **Hang-Seng:** This is a collection of the 50 top-ranked companies listed on the Hong Kong Stock Exchange.

- **NASDAQ Composite:** This is a collection of the world's leading tech companies.

Stock trading has fiercer competition compared to forex. Again, depending on the country where one is based, they might be required to hold a minimal amount of money as capital. In the US, for instance, one should have at least $25,000 in their account. Due to this, trading stocks might be unfavorable for beginners who have limited capital.

3. The Futures Market

Just like the name suggests, the futures market involves making trades for the future. Better put, they are a form of contract where a seller and a buyer agree to execute a trade at a specific date and price in the future. Futures trading mostly involves commodities like precious metals, oil, and foods.

The idea of futures contracts is to minimize risk and unpredictability. For example, if you knew that in a few weeks' time, you would have dug 1 kilogram of gold, you can agree with a buyer to buy it at the current price of gold, as long as it is profitable for you. When you have the gold in hand, you will get the price that you had agreed on whether the price of gold at present went up or fell. In this way, profits are guaranteed, and the risk is minimized.

Similarly, in the futures market, you purchase a financial asset online and only sell it after a specified time or after it attains a specific value in the future.

Just like stock markets, trading futures requires a lot more money than forex and some of the other markets. On average, you need a few thousand dollars to be able to trade, although this varies with the type of future contract that you choose. For instance, you need at least $3,500 to trade the S&P 500. Flexibility is also low since one might be required to close one contract before executing another.

4. The Options Market

Options markets are quite new compared to the three markets above. Options are straightforward financial derivates where a contract allows the trader to buy or sell an instrument within or during a pre-determined time. It is the seller's obligation to fulfill the transaction by either buying or selling their instruments before the set expiration date.

Options trading is considered risky because of the fixed expiration. When executing an options trade, one can either CALL, which means buying at the current price, or PUT, which means selling at the current price.

Examples of tradable options include mini options, index options, stock options, S&P options, and so on. However, some of these instruments might not be possible when day trading.

5. The Crypto Market

The cryptocurrency market is the newest type of online trading. Cryptocurrency refers to digital money that is based on the internet and uses cryptographical functions to enable financial transactions. Since this currency is not regulated, it tends to be rather risky and prone to fluctuations. All the same, it has gained significant popularity recently and continues to rise. Therefore, it can be traded like fiat currencies.

Bitcoin is the most popular and valuable cryptocurrency at the time of writing this book. Other cryptos include Dash, Ethereum, Ripple, and Litecoin. These can be traded similar to the forex markets since they are forms of money; that is, you can make profits by exchanging currency with cryptocurrency.

The cryptocurrency market is becoming a large entity in online trading due to several factors. One of them is due to the high volatility of the currencies. The second one is that trading them requires very little capital, just like forex trading. Another reason is that they are easy to access and can be traded without requiring a broker.

6. The Binary Options Market

The final type of online trading market that we are going to discuss is known as binary options. It is a rather interesting form of trading in that all you need to do is to predict whether an instrument will trade higher or lower after a certain time. Better put, if the current price of gold is $1,500, you can predict that it will be higher or lower after 15 minutes. If your prediction is correct, then your capital grows. If the prediction is incorrect, then you lose the amount you had staked.

Binary options trading is fast emerging as a favorite market for day traders because of the expiry feature. In addition, one can trade on almost any financial instrument across the market. Another advantage of binary options is that the required capital is very little, as some brokers allow the traders to stake a dollar or less per trade. Finally, this is the only market where a person knows how much they can make or lose even before they execute the trades.

CHOOSING YOUR MARKET

As stated earlier, the day trading strategies that we are going to study in this book can be used in any type of market. However, it is up to the individual trader to decide which type of market they prefer to focus on. You can choose more than one type of market, but it might end up being too tedious and confusing. As such, as we go deeper into the book, you might consider trying the strategies for different markets so that by the end of it, you will have made a decision.

Some factors that might help you in choosing your preferred market are:

- **Accessibility:** Make sure the type of market you choose is available in your country, or there are brokers that you can use. The closer a broker is to your country, the better.

- **Resources:** Different markets have different requirements. For example, you can trade binary options from a phone, but stocks and forex are best done using a computer. In short, choose what you can comfortably support.

- **Capital:** This aspect has been mentioned several times already. You should only go for the market that you are sure you can finance without struggling. Forex, crypto and binary options are the best choices if you have little to risk.

- **Volatility:** This is the amount of price fluctuation that an instrument undergoes in a given time. Since we are going to be focusing on day trading, look for markets that move a lot during the day, so you have enough opportunities to make profits.

- **Liquidity:** This is the ability to sell or buy a financial instrument without the price being affected. High liquidity means you can make more trades in a day.

- **Personality:** This is a very important factor to consider when choosing your markets. You might find that stocks are more appealing to you than binary options or futures contracts. Choose what you find interesting as it is your first step toward a successful day trading.

To this point, you should have a clear understanding of what makes up online trading and the different markets that you can go for. It might be too early to choose what you want, but things will clear up as we start doing the actual trading, and you practice on some of these markets. If this is the case, let us find out what day trading means in the next chapter.

CHAPTER 2
WHAT IS FOREX TRADING?

In the previous chapter, we have seen that the forex market is the biggest and most traded one. We would, therefore, not be wrong to conclude that even a majority of those who will download this book might end up trading in this gigantic market. Well, the point we are trying to drive home here is that the forex market will form the basis of our guide. We shall focus primarily on it, bringing out the strategies that will guarantee our success as day traders.

Like we said earlier, in as much as the stock market, the futures market, the options market, the cryptocurrency market, and the other markets are independent types of trading, they all use the same approach. A good example is that all the charts that we shall use for our analysis in forex day trading will contain what we call candlesticks, fundamental analysis, and indicators. These are helpful in reading the markets and understanding where there is a consistent movement of the price (we call it a trend), where the market is likely to bounce and go up (we call it support), and so on. The same tools and approaches are used in analyzing and trading all the other markets.

In stocks, the charts are analyzed using the same candlesticks, indicators, and fundamental analysis. The same happens in the cryptocurrency market. When there is high-impact news, the cryptocurrency markets will be very volatile. The same would happen in the ETF and binary options markets. If we decided to do individual guides for each of the markets that we have, we would not only end up with a humongous book that we would never finish reading; the content would also be repetitive because, for the last time, they all use the same concepts. Therefore, don't think that we have focused too much on forex and left the other markets out.

DEFINITION OF FOREX TRADING

Have you ever exchanged some dollars or any currency for a different currency? For example, you had dollars, and you went to a forex bureau or a bank, and they gave you sterling pounds, Yen, or something else. Maybe you had some cryptocurrency in your online wallet, and you converted it into a currency that you could withdraw and spend physically. If you answered "yes" to any of these, then you have already participated in forex trading. When you took your money to the exchanger, they charged you a little amount then gave you the other currency that you wanted. This is the same thing that happens in the online forex trading market.

In online trading, however, there are a few differences.

- One, you do not exchange physical cash with anybody. Rather, the exchange happens on dedicated trading platforms that we shall discuss later.

- Two, when trading online, you can borrow money from your broker to purchase (or exchange) more currency than what your capital would allow you to.

- Third, you can make as many exchanges as you wish by just clicking a simple button while seated in your living room or cooling off at the beach.

- Finally, unlike when you exchange physical cash and make no profits (in fact, you make losses in terms of what the bureaus charge!), in forex trading, you are the one who will be making the profits. Sounds interesting, doesn't it?

From the explanation above, we can say that forex trading is a form of trading where the currency of one country is quoted against the currency of another. You will see a lot of these side-by-side quotes once we start trading. When exchanging the US dollar with the Euro, we write it as EURUSD. If someone said the price of EURUSD was 1.505, they are simply saying that 1 Euro is equivalent to 1.505 US dollars. Similarly, if they say the price of GBPJPY is 135.10, then it means 1 Euro is equivalent to 135.10 Japanese Yen.

The forex market is interesting because it has no centralized exchange like futures and stocks. We can say that the DAX 30 is based at the Frankfurt Stock Exchange, and the S&P 500 is based in New York, but the forex market has no central place. Rather, it uses a method known as Over the Counter, OTC, which means it is not executed in any regulated environment. The aim of this huge market is to allow a quick and easy channel for countries, governments, central banks, businesses, and other international traders to convert currencies and do business with other nations across the globe.

As you can see, the forex market was not made just so people could trade. Rather, it is meant for big players who need to exchange currencies from time to time. Small-scale traders like us take advantage of the changes in currency rates to make profits by taking views on the direction of the exchange rates. All we need to do is predict whether the exchange rate of a certain quote will increase or decrease, then stand by and watch. Back to the EUR-USD, if the current price is

1.505, and from our analysis, we think the Euro will lose value against the dollar, we use the dollar to buy some Euros. In the market, we call this selling. If the price starts going lower than 1.505, we start making profits, the further it deviates from this figure. On the other hand, if the price starts getting higher than 1.505, then we start making losses.

Conversely, if we anticipate the Euro to gain value against the dollar, we will use the Euro to buy some dollars. This is called buying. If the price starts increasing beyond 1.505, we are going to start making profits, and the higher it goes, the more we make. If our analysis was wrong and the price began getting lower, then we will start making losses, and the lower it goes, the more we lose.

MAIN PARTICIPANTS IN THE FOREX MARKET

Now that you have a clear understanding of what forex trading entails, let us look at the participants. These are the parties responsible for the changes in price every microsecond.

- **The first group of market participants is known as market makers.** In this group, we have international banks that have enough money to create changes in market prices. If they decide to buy a currency, they buy so much of it that its supply in the market reduces, causing it to gain in value. If they sell a currency, its supply in the market gets saturated, causing its value to depreciate. Probably you can see why they are called market makers.

- **The second group is known as multinationals.** It is composed of the biggest companies in the world. This is the group that does the actual exchange of one currency to another since they need different currencies to conduct business with other international firms. In addition to forex, they are also popular in stock trading and the futures market.

- **The third group is known as the speculators.** They utilize the market differently from the multinationals and market makers since their aim is to predict the direction of the market. They make their money by "betting" on possible price directions. In this group, you will find hedge funds, commercial banks, and commodity trading advisors, among others.

- **The fourth group consists of central banks from all over the world.** They are responsible for keeping the economies of their countries stable by regulating their currencies. To achieve this, they manage the way that their currencies are being traded. If they realize there is too much supply of it, they buy it to create demand, thus causing the value to increase. Similarly, if they realize that their currency is being used for speculation, which they hate, they move in to manipulate the market so as to keep the value stable.

- **The final group is known as retailers.** This is where individuals like us, and small-scale trading firms, are classified. We have no ability to manipulate the market, so all we do is predict the movement of price and make profits from it. In a way, we are small-scale speculators. This is the riskiest group since it has no power over the market and is, therefore, prone to sudden market movements caused by the big players. In fact, the big players are known to "hunt" our money when we are trading.

OUR ROLE AS RETAIL TRADERS

Despite being ranked at the lower end of the trading hierarchy, retail traders are so numerous that collectively, they can move the market. The problem is that since there are too many of us, and each one of us understands the market differently, we cannot pile our resources together and move the prices. In short, some of us will be buying, as others sell. Others will be waiting as others are trading. At times, when we are going in, others are exiting. In the long run, we are found all over the place without order.

The above phenomenon makes us the prey of all the big players. Since they have the privilege of being able to move prices, they move prices against us and take our money. Unlike retailers, the big players have more market information, such as where retailers have placed the most trades. If they realize that the trades in that zone are "buy" orders, they execute large "sell" orders, and the retailers end up making losses.

While this might appear like something bad, if you can crack the way the big players see the market, then you can make profits when they make their moves. This is one of the reasons you need quality day trading information, and that is exactly what this book was made for. The strategies that we are going to be studying enable us to know when the price is likely to go higher, go lower, stagnate, and also when to keep off the markets.

We are going to use the same tools that the big players use and try to think as they do. This is called market analysis. In so doing, you will be able to predict when the big boys are about to make a big move that will move prices significantly. In doing so, while uninformed traders will be making losses, you will be flowing with the majority and will be making consistent profits as a day trader.

CHAPTER 3
THE FOUR MAJOR TRADING STYLES

Inside the world of trading, there has been a never-ending debate on whether short-term or long-term trading is the best. Short-term trading, also known as active trading, involves trading for minimal periods of time, ranging from seconds to a maximum of one day. Under this type of trading, we have scalping and day trading. Long-term trading, also known as buy-and-hold trading, involves trading for extended periods of time, ranging from a few days to months and even years. Under this category, we have swing trading and position trading. Traders in both categories claim their style is the best, and they give supporting reasons.

Let us look at the four major trading styles below and later explain why we settled on day trading.

ACTIVE TRADING STYLES

Scalping

The scalping style of trading is the quickest strategy that active traders use. When scalping, a person enters a trade and exits it within seconds or a few minutes. In short, they aim to take advantage of the slightest changes in prices and leave without allowing the risk of time to occur. This style is very popular in binary options and forex markets.

Due to the fast entry and exit times, scalpers make tiny profits. As such, they might need to trade numerous times in a day to achieve any targets or to make enough money. They also prefer very volatile markets with high liquidity since one needs sudden huge price movements to succeed in scalping.

Day trading

The second type of active trading is day trading. This is a type of trade that is opened and closed on the same day; that is, it does not stay overnight. Day trading is the most popular and best-known trading style. Market makers and retail traders are known to prefer this method above the rest.

Unlike scalpers, day traders take more time with their trades, and they can manage them throughout the day. This style of trading is slower and takes advantage of intra-day price movements, which are moderate, although, during major economic events, the fluctuation of prices can be frantic.

BUY-AND-HOLD TRADING STYLES

Swing Trading

Swing trading is the most common strategy in buy-and-hold trading. Here, a trader identifies a trade opportunity, and they hold it for several days before closing it. Their aim is to catch and take advantage of huge price movements, unlike scalpers and day traders. Swing trading requires more experience and patience compared to any form of active trading.

In this trading style, the trader only checks their charts a few times a day. Once a trade has been opened, they only need to check in a few times, maybe twice, to see how their trades are performing. Again, the analysis required for swing trading is more demanding since one has to be able to foresee when a new move is about to occur as well as when it is expected to end.

Position/Trend Trading

The second style of buy-and-hold trading is known as position or trend trading. In it, trades are executed and left to run for weeks, months, or years. The traders use larger timeframes in analyzing their charts to find long-term price directions. Position traders do not like high price fluctuations but a price that moves slowly and gradually toward their direction.

Position trading is mostly used by parties that have huge amounts of money, such as speculators and hedge funds.

ADVANTAGES OF DAY TRADING

Our book title already specified that we are going to be exploring day trading. As such, any trades that you will open, whether in cryptocurrency, forex, binary options, options, ETFs, or futures, will be closed on the same day. I have been trading for well over a decade, and I had to try all four trading styles before settling on day trading. My conclusion was that scalping was too tiresome and risky, not to mention the emotional overload after placing several-second trades. Swing and position trading, on the other hand, was too boring for an impatient person like me who had to pay his bills from trading only.

Here are some of the reasons that I chose to go for day trading:

1. Ease of Getting Started

Day trading only requires a person to have the skills, a computer or smartphone, some little money, and a comfortable workstation. Getting the skills is as easy as finding a mentor who has been in the industry for some time (like you did by purchasing this book) and let them show you the profitable methods. You can also do it through practice and experience by reading tons of books and watching videos. However, this can be time-consuming and expensive since most of the information out there is too vague.

Second, since the trade positions held by a day trader are small, you do not need a lot of money to get started. Swing and position trading aims at riding huge price movements, which also come with the burden of sourcing for enough capital. With day trading, though, all you need is a few dollars, and you will be on your way to earning from trading.

2. Fewer Risks

The second advantage of day trading is that there are fewer risks involved. First, due to the short time required for holding positions, one is advised to risk only a small percentage of their account. In the event that losses occur, only a small amount is lost. Second, in day trading, you can open several positions within a day. As such, if some of the positions become losers, they can be closed and the profitable ones left to run. On the contrary, swing and position traders usually have very few trade opportunities. Therefore, when the trades turn into losers, they have no winning trades to cover the loss.

3. Daily Profits

How does it feel to end every day with your salary already paid? This is possible with day trading. Since all trades need to be closed by the end of the day, you will know how much you made or lost before going to bed. Day traders, therefore, have more peace of mind compared to long-term traders who might need to wait for days or months before knowing the fate of their trades.

4. More Opportunities

Once we start analyzing the charts, you will understand this better. Traders use what we call "timeframes" to analyze their charts. Scalpers use the least timeframes, which might be as low as 1 minute up to 5 minutes. Therefore, in a day, they can find tens or hundreds of opportunities. Day traders use 15-minute charts for up to 1 hour, meaning they get tens of opportunities. When it comes to the larger timeframes, such as daily, weekly, and monthly, trading opportunities might be fewer.

5. Fewer Transaction Costs

In the next chapter, you will learn that brokers charge a tiny amount of money for providing traders with market data and trading platforms. Whenever you make a trade, a little amount is charged. You will notice that some brokers charge an extra amount for trades that stay overnight. As such, a trade that runs for many days will be charged something daily. In the long run, the amount might accumulate and reduce one's profits or capital. Day traders, however, are not charged since they do not have sleepover trades.

6. Familiarity with the Markets

The last advantage of day trading is that due to spending a lot of time on the charts, the learner familiarizes themself with the movements of prices in the markets. In short, they get to understand the individual instruments that they are trading. I have found this to be true since I know how some stocks and currencies behave when the markets open, before important news releases and before prices start to change. All these have helped to increase my earnings and reduce my losses.

DISADVANTAGES OF DAY TRADING

I like to be honest about everything. In light of this, let me reveal that while day trading might appear to be the perfect trading style, it has disadvantages of its own.

Let us look at them.

1. Higher Chances of Making Losses

Day trading can be very risky, especially for unskilled or uninformed traders. Since we make numerous trades within a day, if all of them or a majority of them were losers, it would cause significant harm to your account. Do not worry, though, because this book is meant to make you informed, so you can remain on the profitable side.

2. Tedious

Trading is a very interesting profession since you get to sit down, analyze charts, and watch as your money grows. However, when it is overdone, it can be tedious, just like anything else. Every trade requires proper analysis; so, the more trades that you make, the more likely you are to burn out. This can be avoided by setting specific times for trading and having a few instruments to analyze.

3. Price Fluctuations

The prices of all financial instruments change every microsecond. The rate of change might differ across markets. For example, stocks fluctuate less than currencies. The rate of change becomes more noticeable as one uses lower timeframes to do their analysis. That said, a day trader can be surprised by sudden price fluctuations due to unexpected economic events, and this might lead to losses. On the other hand, swing and position traders are less affected by changes in prices because they use larger timeframes, which fluctuate less.

As we have seen, traders have four trading styles where they can choose from. This can be determined by many factors. In our case, we have decided to go for day trading since the aim of this guide is to help you make a living out of online trading. Day trading is the only style in which you can set daily targets and know how much you will be earning in a month. In addition, it provides you with the chance to recover your losses since it provides tens of opportunities every day. Concisely, if you make losses today, you will still have more opportunities to recover them tomorrow. Swing trading provides fewer opportunities, and this might not be the most suitable trading style to achieve continuous cash flow.

CHAPTER 4

BASIC REQUIREMENTS FOR DAY TRADING

If there is something that I would never get tired of specifying, it is the fact that online trading should be respected as a professional career. You will come across people who trade as a hobby or just for fun, but they have their own reasons. When talking about day trading for a living, we are talking about the person who perceives trading as their sole source of income. That said, a serious trader should possess the skills and necessary tools to be successful in this art.

Let us take a mechanic for our example. The first things a person needs to become a mechanic are will and passion. No one should go into a profession for any reason other than self-motivation and passion. Second, they need to get the skills and knowledge required to take a car apart, troubleshoot problems, and satisfy the needs of their clients so they can be guaranteed to pay. Third, they need the tools to use in servicing, repairing, and upgrading motor vehicles. With these three requirements met, their chances of being successful mechanics are way above average.

Similarly, online day trading has requirements of its own. Make sure you possess the following arsenal before venturing into trading.

1. Mindset

I do not know why you decided to give online trading a try. However, I hope that you have a solid reason because this is going to be a very demanding journey. If you can recall what I said at the beginning, online trading is not easy. You will have to put in hundreds of practice hours, intense research, and unending education. Therefore, the first tool that you require as a day trader is the proper mindset.

One aspect that you should embrace is that trading is not a get-rich-quick scheme. You will have to build experience and practice a lot before you can start making money like the big players who probably inspired you to pursue this interesting career.

Second, and very importantly, be ready to fail numerous times before you finally crack it. Trading is like an investment game where tricks of all manners will be put into use. You will make mistakes that will lead to losses, but with time, you will understand the rules of the game ad that is where your success will begin. In short, you need a fighting mindset.

2. Education

I believe you already have the first requirement, judging by how far you came in search of this knowledge. You are now onto the second requirement, which is education. A trader needs to know how to trade. This book is an example of the education that you need. There is no point in elaborating this point any further.

3. A Computer

You can use several devices to learn to trade, as well as to do trading, such as computers, smartphones, tablets, and so on. Personally, I would recommend a computer because of the analysis part. You will be opening charts of the trading instruments that have a lot of graphical details. In this case, a big display will allow you to see even the smallest details clearly. In addition, mobile versions of the trading platforms are simplified, meaning some of the tools might be missing.

A simple computer will do. It only needs to have a big display of about 21 inches. I started out with a 17-inch monitor, and it worked well for me. However, when I graduated to a bigger screen, I could see more of the charts, and it simplified my analysis. Here is a summary of the minimum specifications that your computer should have:

- Windows, Mac, or Linux operating system

- Intel i7 processor and above

- Minimum 500GB of hard disk capacity

- 32GB of RAM

Note: These are only my recommendations. You can use a computer with different (lower) specifications, and it might just work out well. Second, you can use two monitors such that one screen will be used for the analysis, and the other one can be used for placing the orders. This is optional.

4. Stable Internet Connection

This is where you do not have too many options. Internet connection quality is very important in online trading as it is the channel through which you receive market data, place trades, and connect with your broker. Therefore, make sure your internet is fast and reliable. Any disconnection or delay can give wrong charting information or even lead to losses during trading.

5. A Broker

A broker is a party that will give you a trading platform, allows you to deposit and withdraw money, and also provide you with trading market data. There are thousands of online trading brokers today. In this area, too, you need the best broker. They must be genuine, trustworthy, reliable, and accessible.

6. Charting Software

Charting Software is also known as a trading platform. This is the application where analysis is done, and orders are executed, as well as managed. There are different types of charting software that you can use. We shall look at the installation of some main ones before delving into the strategies.

7. A Trading Plan

A trading plan is also known as a strategy. This is one of the most important tools in your trading arsenal. The trading plan acts as a guide in helping a trader to make proper trading decisions. It can be summarized as a personal trading constitution, as it contains the rules that govern everything that a trader does in their line of work. This will also be discussed toward the end of the guide.

8. A Trading Account

You will need a good trading account. This is the central point from where you will access the trading platform, connect with your broker, deposit and withdraw your funds, and so on. You need an email address, a phone number, and a few documents, such as a scan of your ID, a recent bank statement, and a utility bill containing your address.

Before creating a real account that will ask for the mentioned documents, you can open a demo trading account. This is a trading account used for practice pur-poses. You are provided with free money, although you cannot withdraw it. A demo account works like a real trading account, only that you do not need to deposit your own funds. Most brokers provide demo accounts for free. We shall go through the steps of opening a trading account when installing the trading platforms.

9. A working station

Finally, now that you have committed to becoming a day trader, it is time to set up an office. First of all, your computer needs a table or desk. Next, you need a comfortable ergonomic chair since you will be seat-ed throughout your working sessions. It is advisable to make the workstation as comfortable as possible as this influence might your mood. A neat, well-lit work-station will not only motivate you to work but also make the working day enjoyable. Add some colored lighting, fluffy carpets, polished furniture, soothing music, or just anything that you feel will enhance your working environment.

With all the above tools, you will be armed, ready to ex-perience the world of online trading. Please remember that you can substitute any of these tools with some-thing different for your convenience. However, if you can find them exactly as I have outlined them or better, you will have a smooth time learning and eventually working as a day trader.

CHAPTER 5
TERMINOLOGY

Online trading has unique phrases and brief terms that are commonly used in communicating by traders. These words are very specific to this profession that they may appear as jargon to non-traders or traders who have not taken their time in learning them. It can be both risky and unprofessional to start trading without getting to understand the meaning of the terms that are commonly used terms in any field.

You do not have to memorize them. I would recommend that you understand what they mean, as this will help you internalize them better. As we go along the day trading journey, we shall be using them, so by the end of it, their meanings will be at your fingertips. Again, these terms are shared across any type of trading that you might look into.

ARBITRAGE

This is a method of trading where one takes advantage of price differences between two financial instruments. In stocks, for example, a share might be selling for $29 in one market and $32 in another. A trader can buy the share in the cheap market then sell it immediately in the secondary market to make a profit of the difference ($3).

ASK PRICE

This is also known as the "offer price." It refers to the price or value at which a seller is willing to accept for an instrument. If you place a EUR-USD trade at 1.234, that is your ask price.

ASSET

An asset refers to the instrument that is being traded. If a trader is focusing on stocks, their assets are all the shares of companies that they can trade. In crypto trading, Bitcoin and all the other cryptos are the assets.

AT THE MONEY

This is also known as "break-even." It happens when, at the end of a trade, or during the closure of a particular trade, the value of the asset being traded is the same as the asking price (opening price). Usually, at break-even, the trader neither makes a profit nor a loss.

BASE CURRENCY/COUNTER CURRENCY

In forex, cryptocurrency, and binary options trading, the assets are expressed as currency A/currency B. Examples are EURUSD, BTCUSD. The currency on the left is known as the "base currency," while the one on the right is called the "counter currency."

BEAR MARKET

A bear market is a term used to define a downward movement of the price or value of an asset. This is when traders open "Sell" trades.

BID PRICE

This is the price or value that a buyer is willing to pay for the acquisition of a trading asset. When placing a trade, the ask price is quoted, as well as the bid price. There is usually a small difference between the two, which the broker keeps as profit.

BONUS

A bonus is any type of incentive or gift that a broker might offer their clients. It can also be referred to as a promotion. Once you start trading, you will see brokers offering all types of bonuses to lure or appreciate their clients.

BOUNDARY

This term is common in binary options. It refers to the time allowed before an asset being traded expires. In short, if you predict that the value of a stock will go higher within 10 minutes, this time is known as the boundary.

BULL MARKET

A bull market is the opposite of a bear market. It is the moment when the value or price of a market seems to be going up. During bullish markets, traders will mostly be placing "Buy" trades.

COMMODITY

A commodity is a type of trading asset that involves raw materials such as metals (silver, gold, copper, etc.), natural fuels (oil and gas), and major agricultural products, such as livestock, cocoa, and coffee.

CURRENT RATE

This is the present value or price of an asset.

EARLY CLOSURE

Just like the phrase sounds, it refers to the ability to exit a running trade immediately without delay.

EXPIRY

This is the date or time when an open trade is scheduled to be closed. It is at this point that the results of trades are determined.

EQUITY

Equity is the alternative name for investment, deposit, or capital that is available in a trading account.

GAP

A gap is a significant difference between two quotes; it is usually unrecorded on the trading charts. It can be explained as a "space" where the values of an asset were not captured. Gaps are common during sudden market movements or during weekends and public holidays when the markets are closed.

INDEX

An index (plural "indices") is a method of grouping several assets or securities under one group, so their performance can be measured as one unit. A good example is the FTSE, which is the measure of the top 100 capitalized firms at the London Stock Exchange.

IN THE MONEY

This means that a trade is making profits, or it has closed at a profit.

LEVERAGE

Leverage is one of the most crucial terms used in trading. It is a feature provided by brokers where a trader can "borrow" some money from them to place bigger trades than their actual capital can allow. It is expressed in ratios such as 1:50, meaning for each dollar that a trader holds, they can "borrow" fifty times more from the broker to place bigger trades that can offer bigger returns. Leverage is as risky as it is interesting since it can magnify losses.

MARGIN

Margin is the amount of money that is required to sustain an open trade. If a trade makes losses, it uses more margin and causes a reduction in the available equity. When the equity gets exhausted, the open trade or trades are terminated.

MARKET PRICE

The market price refers to the real value of an asset as provided from the main market at a specific time.

ORDER

An order is a transaction that a trader places. In short, when you open a buy or sell order, you have placed an order. Call and Put are also examples of orders in options trading.

There are two main types of orders:

- **Opening orders**

Opening orders are the actions intended to execute (open) a new trade. There are different types of opening orders.

  » *Market Order:* An "open" market order means that when the trader presses the button to enter a trade, it happens immediately at the current market value.

  » *Buy-Stop:* A Buy-Stop order happens when a trader analyzes the market and concludes that, after the price or value reaches a certain point in the future, it will go higher. Therefore, they place a pending order at the chosen point. Then when the market reaches it, a "buy" order is automatically opened.

  » *Sell-Stop:* A Sell-Stop order is the opposite of a Buy-Stop order. The trader places a pending order in a future position; then, when the market value hits it, a "Sell" order is automatically opened.

» **Buy-Limit:** A Buy-Limit order happens when a trader analyzes their charts and concludes that when the market falls to a certain point in the future, it will stop falling and start going up. Therefore, they place a pending, and when the market reaches it, a "Buy" order is automatically opened.

» **Sell-Limit:** A Sell-Limit order is the opposite of a Buy-Limit. However, this time, the trader has concluded that when the market value reaches a certain level in the future, it will stop rising and start trading lower. As such, they place a pending order, and when the market touches it, a "Sell" order is automatically opened.

• **Closing orders**

Closing orders are the actions intended to close active (running) trades. There are four types of closing orders. They are:

» **Market Order:** A "Close" market order means that when the trader presses the button to exit a trader, it is executed immediately.

» **Take-Profit:** A Take-Profit order is used to automatically close a trade that is in profit. The trader first opens a trade and then sets a Take-Profit level. When the profitable trade gets to the pre-set level, it automatically closes the trade and keeps the profits.

» **Stop-Loss:** A Stop-Loss order is used to automatically close a losing trade. The trader first initiates a trade and then places a Stop-Loss level in the future. If the losing trade gets to that level, it automatically closes the trade and stops further losses.

» **Trailing Stop:** A Trailing Stop order is an automatic type of order that seeks to book and protect a trader's profits. As such, it only works for trades that are already on the profit side. To set it, a trade decides on a number of pips or points, after which the Trailing Stop is to be launched. Let's say you have a trade that is already 30 pips in profit. You can set a 10-pip Trailing Stop, meaning that after the trade has made 20 pips of profit, it will place a stop-loss order at 10 pips of profit. After another 10 pips of profit (40 pips), it will automatically move the stop-loss at 20 pips. If the market reverses and hits the stop-loss, the trade is closed, and the profits are kept.

OUT OF THE MONEY

This means that an active trade is on the losing side, or a particular trade has been closed at a loss.

PIP

A "pip" the acronym for "point in percentage" is mostly applied in the forex market. It is the measure, in points, of the distance that the value of an asset moves. For instance, if the rate of the USDJPY moves from 135.60 to 135.40, then we say it has moved 20 pips down.

SLIPPAGE

Slippage is an occurrence that happens during the opening and/or closing of a trade where, due to the fast movement of the market, the resulting value differs from the intended one. For example, you want to place a gold versus US dollar trade (XAUUSD) when the market price is 1500. After you press the button to open the order, there is a sharp, sudden movement in price, and the order gets placed at price 1502. In this case, we say there has been a slippage of 2 points or pips.

SPREAD

The spread is the difference between the ask price and the bid price. It is the amount, in pips, that a broker charges for each trade. So, if the market price of an instrument is 120 and the broker provides an ask price of 121 of which you agree to buy it at 122, then the spread in that trade is (122-121) = 1 pip.

SWAP

A swap is a charge that occurs when one currency is exchanged for another. It is common in the forex market and usually happens at midnight. If the value of the currency that you have bought has gained against the value of the currency that you are selling, then you are paid a little sum by the broker. If the opposite occurs, then you pay the broker a little sum.

QUOTE

A quote, mostly used in currency trading, is the expression of the base currency versus the counter currency. As such, XAUUSD, GBPUSD, and EURUSD are all examples of quotes.

Speaking the language of online trading is the first step toward being successful. You need to be conversant with what the most important terms in the industry mean. This way, your study and practice will be flawless. The above list of common terminology used in trading is not conclusive; there are countless more. However, they are enough to help you get started. As your time spent in day trading increases, you will come across thousands of other words that we use. Please refer to this chapter any time you find unclear words in your trading journey.

CHAPTER 6

TRADING PLATFORMS

D ay traders have a variety of trading platforms to choose from. A trading platform is a program or software that a trader uses to access market data, conduct their analysis, and place trades. There are tens of available platforms in the market. Recently, due to the growth of the trading industry, more options have been introduced, and competition has become stiff. At the end of the day, it is up to the trader to decide on the platform or platforms to use.

PLATFORMS YOU COULD USE

In this section, we are going to discuss some of the most popular platforms available in the market. You can consider the features we are going to discuss as a filter to help you in choosing your best platform. All the same, I will recommend the one platform that I have used all my life.

MetaTrader 4 (MT4)

MT4 is one of the oldest trading platforms in the industry. It is one of the programs that led to the growth of retail traders as it enabled them to access the market. Traders find it highly reliable and easy to use, making it the most popular trading platform in use for decades now. I personally prefer it over any other platform for several reasons such as:

- It is highly stable.

- It supports a lot of indicators, trading instruments, and robots.

- It can work on all mobile and computer operating systems.

- It is available in almost all brokerage companies.

- It is free.

MetaTrader 5 (MT5)

Just like the names suggest, MT4 and MT5 are related since they are made by the same company (Metaquotes). Their major difference is that the MT5 platform is more advanced and includes more features than the MT4. For instance, the MT5 is even more stable. It is faster, holds more robots and indicators, and also comes with more trading instruments.

It is advisable that even if you start out with MT4, you should gradually transition to MT5 as the older platform may stop being used in the future. We are going to base our learning on this newer trading platform. You can also use the MT4 as they operate the same way.

Ninja Trader

The Ninja Trader platform is quite young compared to the MT4. It came into the market in 2004. All the same, some traders prefer it over the MT4. While the MT4 is mostly suitable for trading currencies (forex and cryptocurrency), the Ninja Trader readily supports forex, stock, and futures trading. In addition to this, the platform offers trade simulation, automated strategy development, and advanced charting tools and abilities. Some disadvantages of the Ninja Trader that keep the MT4 in the lead include:

- Users must buy a license or lease the platform to be able to execute trades.

- Plug-ins like indicators and robots are not free.

- It is not a market data provider, so traders must connect to a data provider like Kinetick or Google.

cTrader

The cTrader software comes third after the Metaquotes platforms and Ninja Trader. It has been displaying stiff competition in recent years, and many brokers have been taking it up. Some of the features that make it highly competitive include fast trade execution, cheaper costs of trades, vast device support, and advanced charting capabilities. However, unlike the other platforms, it does not support Windows Phone OS.

ProRealTime

ProRealTime is a web-based platform (it does not need to be installed on a computer) as it is backed up on the cloud network of the company. It uses a unique coding language (ProRealCode) to create market analyzing tools. While this feature makes it unique, it also means there are fewer tools available online. Another disadvantage is that users must pay to use the platform and access real-time data.

eSignal

eSignal might not be the most popular trading platform, but it is a favorite tool for advanced traders who prefer to customize their own trading approaches. Once a trader learns the supported coding language, they can create their own indicators, trading strategies, and other analytic tools. In addition, eSignal allows a trader to view over 500 trading instruments at a go.

On the downside, traders must pay annual or monthly fees to gain access to market feed. Second, the platform is not common in most brokerage companies.

Remember, it is up to you as the trader to decide on the type of trading platform to use. In our case, though, we are going to use the MT5 as it is user-friendly and contains all the necessary tools, instruments, and features that a trader needs.

INSTALLING THE TRADING PLATFORM

The trading platforms are available on the brokers' websites. You need to sign up with a broker of your choice before accessing any trading platform. Once registered, the broker will provide you with a list of all the trading platforms that they support for you to choose from. The installation process is quite simple and usually requires filling in some personal details and other information that will be provided by the broker.

In our case, we shall be using the MT5, which is very similar to the MT4 platform. The MT5 is very easy to install. To make it even better, we can use the platform for learning purposes without signing up with any broker. However, this will only be a demo account. To access the MT5, head over to the Metaquotes website, and download the MT5. I recommend this method because you will not have to undergo the long process of applying for an account. You can do this when you are ready to use a live account.

Once you have downloaded the MT5 file to your computer, run it and make sure your internet is active. When the installation is complete, a window like the one below should open up.

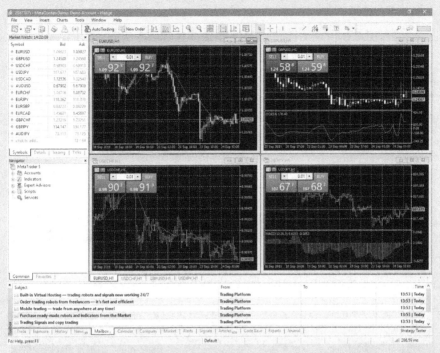

*The MT5 platform. **Source**: Metaquotes MT5*

If you successfully get to this point, then you are ready to start your journey to successful day trading.

Note: Let me remind you that the MT5 platform can be used to trade stocks, futures, and forex (including cryptocurrency). Therefore, even though we shall be using a forex chart for the lessons, remember that the appearance, operation, and analysis are the same in the other markets. As such, you can apply the lessons that you will get here to trade in any of the other markets.

TYPES OF CHARTS ON MT5

Now that you have the trading platform ready, let us look at the types of charts that you can use. The four windows with a lot of graphics that you can see above are known as charts. Let us look at the three types of charts that we can use for analyzing the market.

Line Chart

To activate a line chart, you need to first select one of the charts in the open windows. In my case, I have chosen the EURUSD chart. You can see the title of the charts on the top-right corners. Once you have chosen your chart, click on the "Line chart" icon at the top of your MT5.

You should end up with a chart like this one:

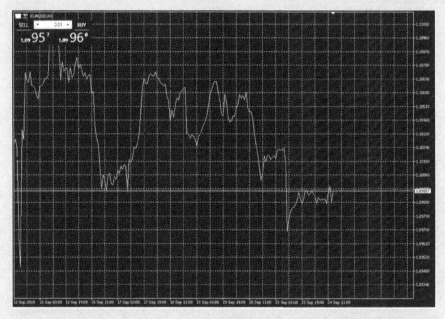

A line chart

You will see a green line in the resulting chart. That line is called an indicator. We shall look at them later, but for now, you need to get rid of them. To do so:

- Right-click inside the EURUSD chart

- Go to the "Indicator List" option and click it

- You will see "Moving Average." Click it and press "Delete."

Your line chart will now be plain.

So, what you are now looking at is called a line chart. This is a simple graphic that represents the movement of prices. When it is sloping upward, it means the price was increasing, and when it slopes downward, it means the price was decreasing.

Bar Chart

To activate a bar chart, you need to click on the "Bar chart" tool at the top of your MT5.

You should end up with a chart like this one:

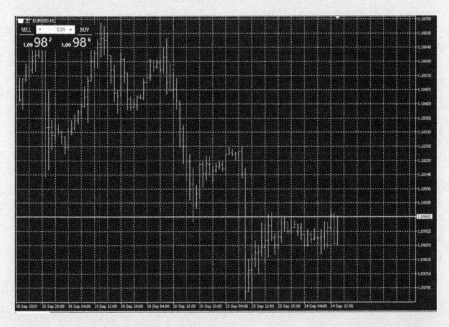

What you are looking at is right now is a bar chart. Unlike a line chart, the bar chart has more details. It shows the opening and closing of prices. You will see that there are vertical lines with tiny horizontal lines on either side. They are called "hashes." The hashes on the left show the opening prices, while those on the right show the closing prices. The top of the bars represents the highest point that price went, while the bottom part shows the lowest point that price touched.

A single bar represents time. Inside the charts, next to the name of the currency pair, you can see the label "H1," which means that each bar in the chart takes 1 hour to form. You can change the timeframe, and see the formation of bars for every 1, 5, 15, 30, 60 minutes up to 1 month by choosing any of the times shown in this frame:

Bar charts are also known as OHLC charts where 'O' stands for the opening price, 'H' for the highest point that price went, 'L' for the lowest point, and 'C' for the closing price of the bar.

Candlestick Charts

Candlestick charts are the most interesting charts. They use bars that look like candles with wicks to show the performance of price. Just like bar charts, they also show the open and closing prices, as well as the highs and lows of prices. However, they look different in that they have wider bodies and single lines on either side called 'wicks.' Candlestick bars are also colored to represent prices going up or down within a selected timeframe.

To activate a candlestick bar, click the "candlesticks" icon next to where you found the line and bar chart icons.

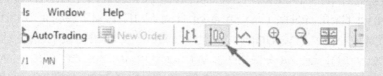

You should end up with a chart like the one below:

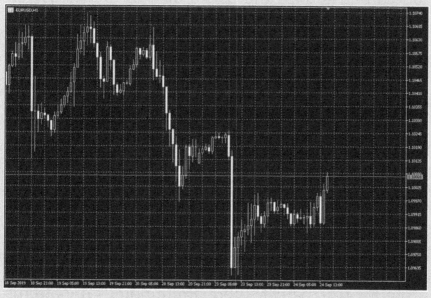

A candlestick chart

As you can see from the chart, some bars have white bodies and green wicks. These ones show that within that time (1 hour), the price of the EUR-USD went down. The price opened at the top of the white body and closed on the opposite end of the white body. The green wicks on top of the white body show the highest point that the price reached before coming down, while the ones on the opposite side show the lowest point that the price reached before going up again. These bars are also known as "bearish candles."

The other candles have black bodies and green wicks. These candles showed when the price went up. In short, during that hour, the rate of the EUR-USD went higher. The wicks on the upper side show the highest point that price went before falling, while the wicks on the lower side show the lowest point that price went before rising again. These candles are also known as "bullish candles."

You can customize the colors of the candles as you wish. In most cases, bearish candles are filled with red color, while bullish ones are filled with green. However, the colors have no effect on one's trading; they only help one to see price behavior more clearly.

In our trading journey, we shall be using candlestick charts, just like the majority of traders do. Here are a few reasons for this decision:

- First, due to their shapes and color, it is very easy to interpret what price is doing. A red bar will instantly tell you that the price went lower within a certain time.

- Second, and very importantly for traders, candlesticks form patterns that we can use to interpret and predict the market. There are hundreds of patterns formed by candlesticks as the market moves, and by understanding them, one can become a successful trader. We shall look at the most important patterns in the next chapter.

Before this chapter, you probably heard the word "charting" and wondered what it meant. Hopefully, now, you know what charts are in the trading industry. With that knowledge in mind, it is time to put it to work by discussing market analysis.

CHAPTER 7

MARKET ANALYSIS

After all the theories and information that you have been reading, market analysis is where your actual trading journey starts. The analysis is the process by which traders study the charts and use the knowledge in making decisions about their trades. We say that market analysis is not part of trading; it is the whole essence of trading.

This is another controversial context in the trading industry because traders never seem to agree on which, between the two major types of market analysis, is best. There are actually three types of market analyses. However, only two of them are popular since the third is usually a personal method. So, what are these three types of chart analysis?

They are:

1. Fundamental analysis

2. Technical analysis, and

3. Sentimental analysis

Let us look at what each one of them entails.

FUNDAMENTAL ANALYSIS

Fundamental analysis is a type of market analysis that tries to derive the underlying value of a financial instrument or asset by studying and assessing economic data. In this approach, the traders do not need to look at the charts to determine the future of the market. Rather, they seek all the relevant data about the instruments they are trading and then use the information to make their trades. Some of the economic data that traders look at closely include inflation, employment, GDP, exports, imports, interest rates, central banks' activities, and so on.

The objective of fundamentalists is to use economic reports as indicators to predict the overall conditions of the market. Out of this analysis, they hope to spot trading opportunities that promise high returns and minimum risk. In a nutshell, fundamentalist traders interpret present economic data and then use the information to decide whether an instrument is likely to gain or lose value in the future. For instance, they know that if a report comes out about Facebook launching a new product and the public is highly anticipative of it, the value of the Facebook share (stock) is likely to appreciate in the future. As such, they will buy stocks in anticipation of the growth in value.

Here are some of the economic data that fundamentalists focus on.

- **The economy**

The status of an economy directly affects the value of a country's currency, imports, exports, and other factors. If a country's economy is doing well, then its currency will grow stronger. Its exports will cost more, and the imports will be cheaper. For instance, when the price of oil increases, the value of all the currencies that produce and export the commodity will grow. Similarly, if the growth of an economy is reported to have dropped, the value of its currency and export commodities will decrease.

- **Political stability**

Political stability leads to increased confidence in the commodities or currencies of independent countries. On the other hand, political instability erodes investor confidence, leading to less investment and deterioration of economic performance. A good example was in 2018 when Facebook was entangled in the Cambridge Analytical scandal, where it was accused of interfering with the electoral process in Kenya, an East African country. On the first day of the report, Facebook shares lost close to $18 billion. By the time the scandal had stabilized, the company had lost over $134 billion. In this case, any trader that had sold the stock made a lot of money.

- **Government policies**

Government policies, such as interest rates, have significant effects on the general performance of currencies and commodities. When interest rates are increased, this curbs inflation and slows economic growth. Similarly, reducing interest rates stimulates economies by promoting investment. Other aspects, like fiscal policies, also affect the movement of the market. For example, high taxation slows economic performance and discourages business.

- **Observing market makers**

There are traders who wait for the big players in the market to make their moves; then they will jump in and flow with the tide. They base their decisions on the assumption that the big players have the ability to move the markets. If they can spot the big moves as they start, then they can reap big profits. Such traders will, therefore, place their focus on hedge funds, governments, central banks, and other huge financial institutions.

- **Reports and news events**

Do you remember 9/11? If so, then this point will be easy to understand. When the tragic news went live, the dollar plunged immediately. In about 5 days, the US economy had lost over $1.4 billion. In this case, anyone who had bought the EUR-USD would have made a lot of money. Similarly, any trader who had sold the USD-JPY would have made handsome profits as well.

Another event is when, in 2019, a Boeing 737 MAX crashed in Ethiopia a few months after a similar plane had crashed in Indonesia. Both flights killed all the passengers and crew. Controversy emerged that the plane model was unsafe. In just a few days, the shares of Boeing sunk by 12%, which is close to $27 billion from the market. A trader who had analyzed this event and sold the Boeing stocks would have made a lot of money from the decline in price.

Do you now understand how fundamental analysis works?

Advantages of Fundamental Analysis

- First, since fundamentalists seek to predict the movement of the markets before they happen, they can easily explain why a movement occurred. This fact alone is enough to increase one's predictive ability and profits.

- Second, studying economic data can help a trader to know the long-term position of price. In short, they can place trades and know where to anticipate the market to reach in the future. This improves their confidence when they have active trades.

- Third, due to the amount of data that is collected and analyzed, a trader gains a better understanding of the markets. As such, they can predict the markets more accurately and reduce guesswork.

Disadvantages of Fundamental Analysis

- The biggest downside of fundamental analysis is that it lacks definite timing. A trader might know that the price of a stock will decline in the future, but they have no specific time when the fall will start. This is very risky when trading.

- Second, due to the lack of proper timing, this approach is not suitable for short-term trading, such as day trading or scalping. However, there are some types of fundamentals that can be used for day trading.

- The third disadvantage is that collecting too much economic data can lead to information overload. When this happens, the trader is unable to process the information. In the long run, they might make wrong decisions that can lead to losses.

- The final disadvantage is that interpreting economic information might vary. One trader might believe that a market will ascend while another interprets the same data in the opposite direction. A wrong interpretation can lead to inaccurate analysis and losses.

TECHNICAL ANALYSIS

Technical analysis is the approach of analyzing the market using the movements of prices in the past. This approach is usually said to be more of an art than it is a science since it mostly uses observation, as opposed to complex formulas and derivations. This time, unlike in fundamental analysis, the trader relies on the charts found in the trading platforms to make their decisions. They do not need to try and interpret economic data but read what the charts are saying.

The most important tool in technical analysis is price data. Different timeframes will display different information, but, all the same, price data must be used to make the trading decisions. Basically, technical analysis studies past and present actions of price and helps the trader to predict the future behavior of the market. The behavior of price is studied using tools like the candlestick, lines, and bar charts that we saw earlier. This approach will work best where the instrument being traded, be it a stock, index, commodity, currency, futures, or option, has enough liquidity and is not susceptible to external influences.

Technical analysis is based on three major assumptions:

- First, that price behavior supersedes all other information, such as economic data. Technical traders firmly believe that the present behavior of price contains all the information about the market. Also, any new information is captured and shown immediately. Concisely, they do not believe so much in the fundamental approach.

- Second, markets move in observable patterns. Technical traders assert that the market moves in patterns that can be observed and used to predict the future movement of prices. However, one has to be trained to observe the patterns when they form. The most-used observable pattern in trading is known as a 'trend.' A trend is a definite direction (up or down) that price seems to be following.

- Third, in the market, history will always be repeated. This assumption is closely related to the above point in that once a pattern has been observed, it can be expected to continue in a certain direction until the pattern has been completed. Repetition in price patterns can be seen in candlestick patterns, volume, chart formations, and momentum, to mention but a few.

Advantages of Technical Analysis

- By using charts, it is possible to choose any time-frame and focus on analyzing the market for a specific time. This is very important in day trading because we need timeframes that are less than one day to conduct our studies of price.

- Charts are visual tools; therefore, they enable us to see trends. Trends show the overall direction that the price is moving. In short, from a chart, we can see whether a market is bullish or bearish before deciding to buy or sell an instrument.

- The timing feature in the charts helps day traders to plan their working hours. They can decide when to work, when to break, or when to close their trades since they do not have to be carried over past midnight. In fundamental analysis, a trader's trading time is determined by external factors, such as the time when important data will be released.

- Technical analysis is preferred by many traders because it allows for the automation of concepts. Programmers can create automatic tools known as indicators and expert advisors (robots) to help with analyzing the market as well as entering or exiting trades.

- The other advantage of technical analysis is that it easily highlights important zones in the market. For example, you can tell where the market is likely to make a U-turn by looking at the charts. You will read more about this under Support and Resistance.

- Finally, compared to fundamental analysis, technical analysis is less consuming as the trader does not have to pursue different channels of information so they can make their trades. In the latter, we only need to look at the charts.

Disadvantages of Technical Analysis

- Charting is not as easy as it might sound. One reason is that different timeframes can give different signals. A 1-hour timeframe might predict a rising price, while the 15-minute chart shows a falling price. Such occurrences can be confusing.

- There is another issue that is closely related to the above point, known as analysis paralysis. This is where a trader overanalyzes their charts until they get too confused to make a confident decision.

- Third, due to the presence of thousands of automated indicators and robots, different traders might interpret the market differently. Automated systems may not necessarily work the same, thus the varying signals. This can also lead to confusion or wrong analysis.

- Finally, while technical analysts might ignore fundamentals, this approach might have significant influences on their analysis. During major news or events, the market might ignore any formations and patterns that have formed, leading to wrong analysis or losses.

SENTIMENTAL ANALYSIS

Sentimental analysis is not as popular as the two other approaches, but still, it is used by some day traders. Unlike the other two, sentimental analysis is based on the trader's opinion and not on any external factors. In short, the trader will look at the market and provide personal opinions on whether the market is going up or down.

One of the methods used in the sentimental analysis is measuring the ratios between the buyers and the sellers. If the buyers (called 'bulls') are more, the trader is likely to place "buy" trades. On the other hand, if the sellers (called 'bears') appear to be in charge, then the trader is more likely to place "sell" trades.

The sentimental approach is the riskiest of the three. As such, traders usually use it together with any of the two major approaches.

FUNDAMENTAL OR TECHNICAL ANALYSIS?

You are now part of this huge battle since you chose to become a trader!

Well, any seasoned trader will tell you that all three forms of analysis are very important in day trading. The three approaches should complement each other if a trader needs to increase their winning ratio. When one of them is ignored, the risks of making the wrong predictions increase.

Due to the above revelation, we are going to use all three methods. However, technical analysis will be the dominant one. I have chosen the technical approach because day trading needs sharper accuracy compared to position and swing trading. In addition, I find observation to be more revealing than just basing my decisions on verbal information. In my many years of trading, I have come to prove that, indeed, history repeats itself in the markets. You will also realize the same.

The tools found in charts, together with the historical behavior of price, will help us to understand and foretell the potential direction of the markets with significant accuracy. All the same, even as we focus on technical analysis, we shall also include a few important fundamentals and how to utilize them for better gains in day trading.

Next, we look at candlestick patterns.

CHAPTER 8
CANDLESTICK PATTERNS

The candlesticks that we are talking about are actually known in full as "Japanese Candlesticks." They were invented by a Japanese trader and later grew in popularity in the 90s. Since their importance was discovered, Japanese candlestick charts have become the most popular type of trading chart used today.

ANATOMY OF CANDLESTICKS

Japanese candlesticks contain very important information about the market. A trader can read the market like an open book once they understand the anatomy of a candlestick. This is usually the first and very important step toward successful trading. You need to understand what the market or price is doing so you can make appropriate decisions. In this chapter, we are going to break down the candlesticks and understand what each shape and pattern tells us about the market.

Before we start, let me clarify that our bullish candles will have white bodies and black tips, while the bearish ones will have black bodies and black wicks. You can use any color of your preference by changing it in your MT5. To do so, right-click inside your chart window, click on "properties" then adjust the colors as you wish.

Black candlesticks are bearish, and white candlesticks are bullish

Candlestick Bodies

When you look at your charts, you will realize that candlesticks come in different sizes. Some of them are very tiny, while some are huge. These sizes actually mean something!

The short bodies mean there was little buying or selling activity. The short white candlesticks mean that there was little buying activity. The short black candles mean there was little selling activity

On the other hand, long bodies mean there was a lot of buying or selling. Long white candlesticks mean there was a lot of buying activity, and the bulls were in control of the market. Similarly, the long black candlesticks mean there was a lot of selling activity, and the bears were in control. The longer the candlesticks are, the more buying or selling activity was happening in the market.

Candlestick Wicks

The wicks on the candles also have very important information.

The wicks on the upper side of the candlesticks show that the bulls pushed prices high before sellers came in and pushed the price lower. Those on the lower side show that the sellers tried to take the price lower, but the bulls came in and pushed it higher. As a trader, you should always perceive the market as a battle where the bulls are always fighting against the sellers, as they seek to control the direction of the markets.

Long shadows on the upper side of a candle show that there was a lot of buying pressure, and the buyers were in control of the market for some time before the bears came in with more power and lowered the prices. Short shadows on the upper side show that there was no buying pressure, or the bulls were not interested in driving prices past that level.

In the same way, long shadows on the lower side of a candle show that there was a lot of selling pressure from the bears, but the bulls came in with more power, and they raised the prices. Short wicks on the lower side of a candle indicate low-selling pressure or lack of interest in further selling by the bears.

THE MOST POWERFUL CANDLESTICK PATTERNS

Candlesticks are formed by price behavior, which is known as Price Action in trading. These charts can be used as standalone analysis tools or as confirmations for trading signals. Traders also add robots and indicators to candlestick charts to improve their accuracy.

At times, the markets will form interesting candlestick formations that have very important information. Price action traders are always on the lookout for these formations that we shall call "patterns." When these patterns occur, they tell us that the market is about to do something. An existing trend (price direction) can continue or reverse after a special candlestick pattern has formed.

Candlestick patterns can be formed by one or more candles in a sequence. At this level, we are going to look at patterns formed by single, double, and triple candlesticks.

Single Candlestick Patterns

These patterns are made up of a single candlestick that has special anatomy. Here are some of the most important single-candlestick patterns.

Doji

A Doji is the simplest pattern to spot in your charts. It is formed when the price opens and closes at the same level as where it opened. Due to this, a Doji pattern will always look like a simple dash (-). When a Doji has wicks, it will look like a cross, although the horizontal line will vary in position. The fact that the price opened and closed at the same price means that the bulls are bears were equal in strength. In addition, a Doji is neither a bullish nor bearish candlestick. As such, it is seen as a sign of indecision. When it happens, the trader has to wait for other signs to know where the market will move. You will find that the market might reverse or continue strongly in the same direction after a Doji has formed.

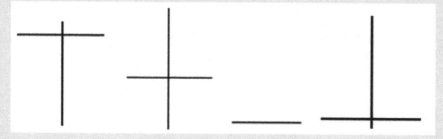

Common Doji formations

Go back to your MT5, and try to find some dojis in the charts. What happened after the Doji?

SPINNING TOP

A spinning top is a candlestick with a very small body and wicks that are longer than the body on either side. Spinning tops indicate intense fighting between the bulls and bears, usually ending in a draw. In short, a spinning top shows that neither buyers nor sellers are in control of the market. Unlike the Doji, a spinning top can be bearish or bullish.

All the same, if a spinning top occurs when the price is moving up (uptrend), it might indicate that the buyers are becoming weaker, and the market might reverse and start moving down (downtrend). Similarly, if it occurs when the price is in a downtrend, it could mean that the sellers are getting exhausted, and that price might reverse into an uptrend.

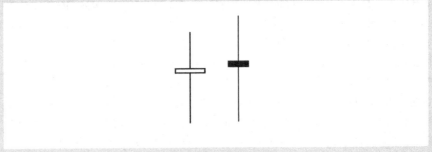

Spining tops

Open your charts and try to find some spinning tops. See what happened in the market after they were formed.

MARUBOZU

Do not mind some of these new candlestick names that you might have never heard before, like *Doji* and *Marubozu*. They are Japanese names, having been coined by the inventor of candlesticks. So, in addition to day trading, you are also learning a little bit of Japanese.

Well, Marubozu is another type of candlestick that is very easy to spot. They appear as candles with bodies and no wicks at all. They can be bullish or bearish.

When a Marubozu appears, it shows that either the buying or selling activity was very strong. A bullish Marubozu shows that the price opened low and went high without being pushed down at all. As such, there were very few sellers, or they were overpowered. In the same way, a bearish Marubozu tells us that the sellers were very powerful that the buyers were not able to push the price any higher.

A Marubozu is considered to be a continuation pattern because, when it happens, the dominant trend at that time continues.

Marubozu candlesticks

HANGING MAN

A hanging man candlestick formation is a bearish candlestick that has a small body, little or no small wick at the top, and a very long wick on the bottom.

When it forms during an uptrend, it might predict a reversal of the trend. In short, the market might start falling. Try to verify this information by looking at where a hanging man was formed during a rising market.

Hanging man candlestick pattern

HAMMER

A hammer candlestick looks like the hanging man, only that it is a bullish candle and is only relevant when it forms during a downtrend. It has a small body with a little or no wick at the top and a very long wick at the bottom.

If it forms during a downtrend, it might be an indication that the trend might reverse, and an uptrend will start.

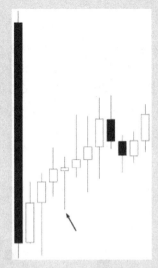

Hammer candlestick pattern

Shooting Star

The shooting star and inverted hammer look like the hanging man and hammer placed upside-down.

The shooting star is a bearish candlestick with a small body, a long wick at the top, and a tiny or no wick on the lower side. This formation is only relevant during a bullish trend, and, when it happens, it is an indication that the trend might reverse.

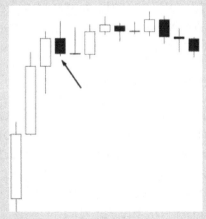

Shooting star candlestick formation

INVERTED HAMMER

An inverted hammer is only relevant if it forms during a downtrend. It is a bullish candlestick that shows a potential reversal of a downtrend to an uptrend. It has a small body, a long upper wick, and a tiny or no wick on the lower side.

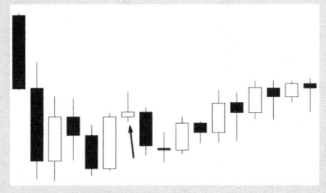

Inverted hammer candlestick

Double Candlestick Patterns

Have you seen the magic that happens after the above single-candle patterns are formed? Yes, they work!

If you have been impressed by the magic of the single-candle patterns, then prepare to be blown away by the power of double-candle patterns. You will realize that the patterns with more candles are more powerful. Let us see if this fact is true.

BULLISH ENGULFING PATTERN

A bullish engulfing pattern is made up of two candlesticks. The bearish candlestick must be on the left side and the bullish one on the right. The distinguishing feature of a bullish engulfing pattern is that the bullish candle should have a bigger body than the bearish one and completely engulf (cover it).

This pattern is only relevant during a downtrend market and will usually imply that the trend might reverse into an uptrend.

Bullish engulfing pattern

BEARISH ENGULFING PATTERN

A bearish engulfing pattern is the opposite of a bullish engulfing pattern. It is formed when a bullish candle on the left is completely covered by a larger bearish candle on the right.

This pattern is only valid when it happens during an uptrend and usually predicts the end of the uptrend and the beginning of a downtrend.

Bearish engulfing pattern

TWEEZER TOPS

A tweezer top pattern is formed when a bullish candle with a small body, small upper wick, and no lower wick appears, followed by a bearish candle with a small body, small upper wick, and no wick on the lower end. In short, the two candles must be similar, only differing in the sense that one is bullish, and the other is bearish.

The pattern is only valid when it occurs during an uptrend and usually signals that the trend is becoming weak and might reverse into a downtrend.

Tweezer tops formation

TWEEZER BOTTOMS

A tweezer bottom formation is the opposite of the tweezer top pattern. It consists of a bearish candle on the left with a small body, no wick at the top, and a long wick on the bottom, followed by a bullish candle with a small body, no wick at the top, and a long wick at the bottom.

A tweezer bottom is only relevant when it forms during a downtrend. It signals a possible end of the downtrend and the beginning of an uptrend.

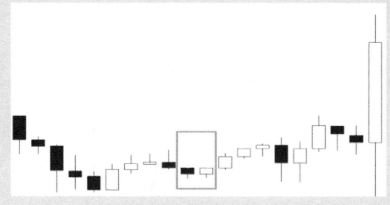

Tweezer bottoms pattern

Triple Candlestick Patterns

As you keep trying to find these interesting candlestick patterns in your charts, you might have noticed that double-candle formations are harder to find. That is true. However, it is more of a good thing because it means that when one of them shows up, something is going to happen in the near future. You should, therefore, be very keen when watching your charts because the patterns are very rare to find and missing out on one means losing a good trading opportunity.

In this part, we are going to look at the most powerful three-candle patterns that we can use in day trading.

EVENING STAR

The evening star pattern is formed by three candles. There should be a good-sized bullish candle (not a Doji) on the left, followed by a much smaller bullish candle in the middle, and on the right, a good-sized bearish candle that is bigger than half of the candle on the left.

This pattern is valid when it forms during an uptrend. It signifies a possible end to the trend and a reversal into a downtrend.

Evening star pattern

MORNING STAR

A morning star formation is the opposite of the evening star pattern. It consists of a good-sized bearish candle on the left, a much smaller bearish candle in the middle, and a good-sized bullish candlestick on the right. The bullish candle must be more than half the size of the candle on the left.

The pattern is valid when it forms during a downtrend. It notifies a trader of a potential end of the downward movement and the possible start of an uptrend.

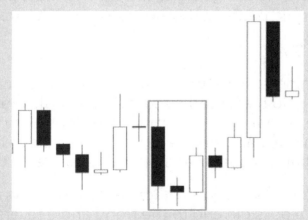

Morning star pattern

Three Bullish Soldiers

The three bullish soldiers candlestick pattern consists of three bullish candles. The first candle should be small, followed by a bigger bullish candle that has a tiny wick at the top, and, finally, a much bigger bullish candle that has tiny or no wicks at all.

This is a reversal pattern that should only be used during a downtrend. When it appears, it signifies that the falling trend is becoming weak, and the bulls are becoming stronger.

Three bullish soldiers

Three Bearish Soldiers

The three bearish soldiers pattern formation is the direct opposite of the three bullish soldiers pattern. It consists of three bearish candlesticks where the one on the left is small, followed by a bigger candle with small wicks then finally a bigger candle with little or no wicks.

This pattern is only relevant during an uptrend. When it is formed, it is an indication that the trend is becoming weak and that a downtrend might begin soon. The growing bear candles show that the sellers are becoming stronger.

Three bearish soldiers

RISING THREE

The rising three candlestick formation is made up of five candles, although only three are the most important. It consists of three small bearish candles sandwiched between two huge bullish candlesticks. The candlestick on the right must close higher than the huge candle on the left.

This pattern is only valid during rising markets (uptrend), and when it occurs, it signifies a continuation of the existing trend.

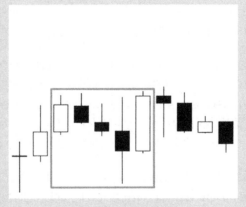

Rising three pattern

FALLING THREE

Just like the rising three candlesticks pattern, the falling three formation is also made up of five candles. However, this time, there are three small bullish candles enclosed within two huge bearish candles. The bearish candle to the right of the pattern should close lower than the first huge bearish candle.

The falling three method is used during downtrends only. When it occurs, it means that the downtrend is likely to continue.

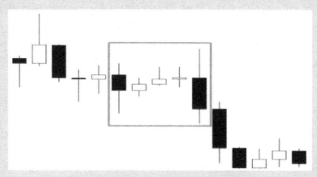

Falling three pattern

SUMMARY

Voila! You have just completed your first charting lesson! How was it? Did you try to find these amazing patterns in your MT5 charts?

Well, candlesticks are the first step toward understanding and analyzing the markets; however, you can use the information that you have already learned to try and trade. I mean, you can now wait for the patterns to form and see how the prices move afterward. We cannot use past formations since the preceding market movements already left us. However, from now on, use the demo Metaquotes MT5 and capital to sell or buy when you see any of these patterns forming.

To place a trade, click on the button at the top-left side of the window where you will see the pattern(s) forming. Click the "Sell" button if you see that a down-trend has formed or the "Buy" button if an uptrend has formed. Keep in mind that you are just getting started, so if you make losses, it does not mean that you are already losing. You still have a long way to go, and the process will only get more interesting.

In conclusion, I hope you enjoyed this lesson and that you were able to find all of the patterns inside your charts. I understand that the three-candle patterns are harder to occur, and that is pretty normal. Feel free to use any tradable instrument on your platform. Like we said in the beginning, the lessons that you will be getting can be applied in any market.

CHAPTER 9

SUPPORT AND RESISTANCE

Any time people are trying to explain trading, they like to advise others to "buy low and sell high." This is a very true and important fact, but the biggest problem is that there is usually no clear explanation on how to find the highs and lows. In this section of the book, we are going to learn how to find the best areas for buying and selling.

Dear reader, welcome to another of trading's most important concepts: support and resistance.

WHAT ARE SUPPORT AND RESISTANCE?

In general, support and resistance zones are the areas in the market where a commodity is expected to exhibit interesting behavior. In most cases, the expected behavior at these zones is opposition. In trading, this opposition is known as "rejection." In short, when the price touches the zones, it might be reversed in the opposite direction. So, if a certain index was rising, when it gets to an important zone of opposition, it might slow down and change into a downtrend. Similarly, a stock that has been moving down might get to a special zone then slow down and turn. At times, the markets choose to be defiant, and they oppose the rejection then move past these important zones.

The market is always a battlefield for buyers and sellers. Just like in any war, each side has its territory, and when the enemy goes closer to their opponent's territory, they risk losing the war. We also have this concept in the market, where the sellers and buyers have their territory. So, at times, the market will go into the sellers' territory, and since they are very strong there, they will send it down. On the other hand, when the market goes near the buyers' areas, they will ambush it by buying heavily. The result will be a rising market.

Support

Support areas are the ones that are below the current position of the market, where the price is likely to slow down, reverse, or take time to break. It is known as a support zone because it attempts to keep the market from going any lower. In these zones, there are many buyers who are waiting for the market to get there, so they can buy it. If you can go back a few lessons back, remember we said that the market tends to repeat its history. Therefore, traders will look at their charts and identify the best support zones then wait for the price to get there. When it does, they will use more analytical tools like reversal or continuation candlestick patterns and then buy once they get the confirmation.

Below is an image showing support zones in a market.

Support zones

From the above image, you can see that when the price reached the support zones, it would bounce and go up. This is because many buyers watch these important areas, and they place buy trades there.

Resistance

Resistance zones are the areas above the current market position where the price is likely to slow down, reverse, or take time to break. They are known as resistance zones since they attempt to prevent the market from going any higher. Resistance areas are the strongholds of sellers. As such, when the market reaches these zones, there are chances that many sellers will execute sell trades and send the market back down. Just like the support zones, traders will identify the areas of resistance then wait for the price to touch them. After this, they can apply more analytical tools, and, if appropriate for them, they will open sell trades.

Here is an image showing resistance zones in the gold market.

Resistance zones

As you can tell from the image, the price would go down after touching the important resistance zones. This is because many traders are always on the lookout at these levels, and, when the price gets to them, they execute sell trades.

Now that you know what the terms support and resistance mean, it is time to go to your charts and mark as many support and resistance zones as you can see.

HOW TO IDENTIFY SUPPORT AND RESISTANCE ZONES

If you did the exercise of identifying these zones in your charts, you probably realized that some of them are very small, while others are big. For the sake of the accuracy and reliability of your trading signals, we are only going to look at the strongest zones.

So, how do we tell when a zone is strong?

Repetition

The first method of identifying the strongest support and resistance zones is looking at how many times the market reached the area and got rejected. Minor zones are touched only once, and then you see that the price broke them later on. On the other hand, the stronger zones are touched by price numerous times, and they reject the price, or it takes multiple attempts before the price eventually moves past them. The more times that a zone is tested by price, the stronger it becomes.

Let us look at an example of a strong resistance zone.

A strong resistance zone

The above image shows a strong resistance area marked by the red rectangle. We refer to it as a strong resistance zone because the market attempted to break it numerous times but failed.

In area 1, we see that the market tried to break it strongly, but the sellers refused to let the price rise any higher. In areas 2, 3, and 5, the market went down immediately; it touched the resistance. In area 4, the sellers were too anxious to sell, and they did it even before the zone was touched.

Note: Support and resistance zones are not lines. Therefore, when drawing them, perceive them as zones (wide areas). Use the rectangle tool in your MT5 to draw the strong zones. To do so, click on "insert," then "objects," then "shapes" choose the "rectangle" option. Click and drag inside the chart to draw your zones.

Here is an example of a strong resistance zone.

A strong support zone

In the figure above, we can tell that the zone is quite strong, as it was tested five times. In areas 1 and 2, the price touched the zone and slowed down. It did not bounce back up or break the zone downward. In area 3, it touched the zone and went up before testing the support zone again at zone 4. Between zones 4 and 5, it slowed down before the bulls initiated a strong up-trend. In this case, we say that the bulls won the war.

Candlestick formations

The second way to identify and validate strong support and resistance zones is by looking at how candlesticks behave when they touch the zones.

REJECTIONS

The most interesting and revealing tell-tale sign that the market has hit a strong zone is that the candlesticks will have very long wicks. If you refer to the two imag-es above, you will see that when the market touches a resistance zone, it mostly forms very long wicks on the upper side. Do you remember what wicks mean? Yes, the long wicks on the upper side mean that the bulls tried to push the price higher, but the bears would not allow them, so they pushed the prices lower.

The same holds for the support zone. You can see that when the price touched it, the candlesticks formed long wicks on the lower side. This means that the bears tried to push the prices lower, but the bulls would not let them. Since this is a bullish stronghold, the bears lost the battle, and the prices went up.

SHORTER CANDLES

Another indication that the prices have hit a major zone is that the candlesticks start becoming shorter (smaller). They have small bodies and wicks. The explanation is quite simple: traders are always looking at the important levels in the market. Therefore, when the price goes near, say, a resistance zone, those who had bought trades close them since they expect prices to reverse. This causes the volume in the market to decrease, thus the minimal trading activity shown by the short candles.

The short candles also show that the bulls and bears are waiting for each other to make a move so they can oppose it. At this time, nobody wants to buy or sell. However, once a definite direction has been established, the candles start growing.

Go back to the above charts and see if this is true. Also, check the areas where you drew the support and resistance zones in your MT4 charts. Does this concept apply? Of course, it does.

To this end, you are now able to identify the strongest support and resistance zones in the market. Next, let us see why these zones are very important in day trading.

USES OF SUPPORT AND RESISTANCE ZONES

Selling High, Buying Low

Finally, you get to understand this overused phrase in the trading industry. It is very simple: when you see the price approaching a support zone, you should always expect a potential bullish move. We say 'potential' because nothing in the market is assured. The price might get to the support zone and choose to slow down, bounce, or break it and continue going lower. What I am trying to say is that you should never be caught buying at a resistance level or selling at an area of support.

It is always advisable to move with the majority of the traders. In fact, big players such as market makers use these points to take our money. Ignorant traders who fail to adhere to this rule usually end up with losses. Concisely, practice hard to identify the strongest zones and wait for the markets to touch them before making any trading decision.

Identifying Market Direction

Market direction, popularly known as "trend" in trading, is one of the most important concepts that you must follow for you to succeed in this industry. Just like you should sell at resistance zones and buy at support areas, you should always trade along the main market direction. You cannot be trying to sell when the majority of traders and the big players are pushing the market up. There is a common phrase that you will hear traders throwing around; that the trend is your best friend.

Many traders hear about this concept, but they fail since they do not understand how to identify the main trend. Luckily for you, this guide will show you the best way to do it.

Now, in the market, there are things known as peaks and troughs. The peaks are the highest points that you can see the market reaching before turning back. Troughs are the lowest points that the market reaches before going back up. Both of these are minor support and resistance points. If you connect the points using straight lines, you will end up with a zigzag formation.

Peaks and troughs

- **Uptrend**

When the peaks are formed in higher succession, we say the market is in an uptrend. If a new peak is formed higher than the previous one, we call it a higher-high. During an uptrend, the troughs are also formed in higher succession. In short, each new trough is positioned higher than the previous one. When this happens, we say a higher-low has been formed. Collectively, when a market is forming higher Highs and higher Lows concurrently, then an uptrend is formed. During this time, you should only look for buy trades.

- **Downtrend**

A downtrend happens when the market starts making lower peaks and lower troughs in succession. In short, when a trough is formed lower than the previous one, we have a descending zigzag direction that we call a downtrend. During a downtrend market direction, lower Highs and lower Lows are formed. In a downtrend, you should only be looking for sell trades.

- **Ranging Market**

There are times when the market is neither moving up nor down. When this happens, it is because it has become trapped between two support and resistance zones. We refer to this as a "ranging" or "sideways" market since price movement is fixed between two points that form a range between them. You might think that since the market is ranging, trading has to stop. Wrong! Once you identify and validate a ranging market, you can take advantage of the movements between the two zones to make some money. However, many seasoned traders advise beginners not to trade ranging markets to avoid being trapped on the wrong side once a breakout occurs.

A ranging market

Confluence

In trading, confluence happens when two or more analytical tools predict the same thing. For example, the evening star candlestick pattern (possible downtrend) may form at a resistance level. In this case, we have two tools that are telling us that the trend of the market that we are looking at might start going down.

Now, support and resistance should be mandatory tools in your trading. Once you have set up the candlestick chart, start identifying the most important support and resistance zones in the market. From there, use the zones to build up confluence. You can look or wait for candlestick patterns to form on the identified levels. A trading signal that is supported by both of these tools increases the likelihood of being profitable.

As you read further, you will get to know more tools that can be used to build up confluence. The more confirmations that you get about a potential trading signal, the more confidence you will gain, not to mention that it might turn out to be a great trading opportunity.

Entry, Exit, Stop Levels

Support and resistance zones are very important when it comes to managing your trades. You cannot go into the market blindly without knowing where you should hunt for trades and where to exit. A real trader needs to know where the market is heading before they execute any trade. In addition, they should be able to tell when the signal that they have taken is wrong so they can exit the trade(s) without incurring further losses.

- ### Entry

Support and resistance help us to know where to expect trading opportunities. We have already discussed this. The first golden rule in entering a trade is to know whether the market is going up, down, or ranging. The second rule is identifying support and resistance zones to know whether you should buy or sell. In an uptrend, only wait to buy when you have a support zone. Similarly, during a downtrend, only wait to sell at a support zone.

- ***Exit***

Before executing a trade, you must know where you expect the market to go. In so doing, you will know where to take your profits and run. Support and resistance will help you to do this. If you have spotted a buy trade, you should expect to get out when the market approached the next level of resistance. You do not want to stay in a trade for too long such that the market gives you profits, then it hits an area of resistance and falls back to take them all back.

Therefore, mark the possible reversal points of the market using support and resistance zones. You can place your take-profits at these levels or manually wait for the prices to get there, then you can exit the trades manually.

- ***Stop Levels***

At times, you will analyze the market and spot a potential trade signal. Unfortunately, once you are already in the trade, the market will not go as per your anticipation, and you will start making some losses. This is normal in trading, and you should accept it. What matters is that you should make more profits than losses. We shall cover this topic wider under Risk Management later in the guide.

So, when a trade has turned against us, and we start making losses, what do we do? Should we let it run and hope that it will favor us later, or do we exit the trade immediately?

The answer is none of the above.

For one, we can never be too sure about the direction of the markets, as they are influenced by hundreds of factors that we cannot control. As such, before executing a trade, we must know where to place our stop-loss. If you recall what a stop-loss is, it is a type of order that automatically closes a losing trade when a trade goes against a trade.

Traders use previous support and resistance levels to place their stop-loss. So, let us assume that you have spotted a potential sell trade that has formed a confluence between a resistance zone and a bearish engulfing candlestick pattern. You will place your stop-loss a little distance above the resistance zone that you are using to trade.

Here is an image for a better explanation:

Entry, exit, and stop-loss using support and resistance

In the figure above, we can see from the extreme left that the market was moving in a downtrend since it was forming lower Highs and lower Lows. At point 1, we drew a resistance when the price reached the zone, and a rejection candle was formed. The market went down and later came to touch the zone again. Let us assume that we had been watching the market all that time.

At point 2, the market formed a bearish engulfing pattern after touching the resistance level. As such, we had a good confluence point here. So we decided to take the trade after the engulfing pattern was formed, and the candle had closed (point 3).

As we opened the trade, we were sure that it was during a downtrend, so the price was likely to go down. As such, we placed our stop-loss (5) near the next important support zone since we expected the price to pause or reverse there.

Similarly, we placed a protective stop-loss above the sell order and the resistance zone that gave us the trade (point 4). This is to close the trade in case the market broke past the zone and formed an uptrend. Please note that the stop-loss is placed beyond the resistance zone to prevent it from being executed in case the buyers attempt to push prices higher and get rejected.

Note: The stop-loss should neither be placed too close to the zone nor too far from it. If placed too close, it might be activated too early and lead to unnecessary losses. It should be allowed a little distance to allow the market some breathing space. Similarly, placing it too far from the zone can lead to excess losses.

If we had taken that trade, you could see that it went down immediately after the bearish engulfing pattern and into the support zone down below. It would have reached our take-profit order, and that would have made it a winning (profitable) trade since it hit the target and not the stop-loss. We won!

SUMMARY

I hope you enjoyed yet another interesting lesson on chart analysis and finding the best trading opportunities. You now have two lethal weapons in your trading arsenal: candlestick formations, as well as support and resistance. I cannot stress enough how important these two concepts are in any form of trading. You already have enough tools to start day trading! All the same, in the next chapter, we shall look at more tools that can help with better chart analysis and identifying profitable trading opportunities.

In the meantime, put the skills that you have acquired so far to use. Draw those zones and wait for candlestick patterns to confirm the trades for you. When you spot a qualified signal, do not hesitate to take it. More importantly, make sure you know where to place your take-profit and stop-loss orders.

CHAPTER 10
CHART INDICATORS

In the past two chapters, we have looked at two major concepts that can be used in analyzing the market and using price action to enter trades, as well as manage. Before we look at more day trading strategies, we need to study a special group of chart analysis tools known as indicators.

Indicators are automated tools that are applied in the charts to reveal information that can be hard to spot with the naked eye. The indicators appear in different shapes and sizes on top of the charts in the trading platforms. We need indicators because charts show much more information than just support and resistance zones or reversal and continuation of trends. As such, by using automated tools, our analysis can improve.

While indicators are meant to enhance one's trading accuracy and confluence, they should never be used as the sole analytical tools. One of the worst mistakes that newbie traders make is applying as many indicators in their charts as they can and using them to make their trading decisions. Do not make this mistake. You should base all your trading on pure price action, which is studying market formations using support and resistance, trends, and candlestick patterns. When it comes to indicators, only use them to build more confluence or reveal hidden information that you can interpret to make better trading decisions.

TYPES OF INDICATORS

If you ever went out there to look for indicators, you would never have enough time and space to store them because there are millions of them. Your trading platform will come with some pre-installed ones. These are very basic ones, but they show the most important information so you might not need to go looking for more. In fact, the basic indicators are the ones used as reference points in the making of the other indicators that you will find being sold or freely available online.

No matter how many indicators we have in existence, all of them can be classified into four categories, namely trend, volume, momentum, and volatility indicators. The indicators in the four groups can be further classified into two groups of either lagging or leading indicators

A lagging indicator is one that shows information that has already passed. For instance, a lagging indicator can show that a reversal has already happened. On the other hand, a leading indicator tries to predict the future price behavior of the market. For example, a leading indicator can tell us that a trend is about to end.

The four main types of indicators are:

- **Trend**

Trend indicators try to reveal the direction of the market (trend) or if there is no movement at all. If used properly, trend indicators can help a trader to know which direction to trade in or whether to stay out of the market.

Some examples of trend indicators are the moving average, Ichimoku Kinko Hyo, parabolic SAR, and MACD.

Trend indicators are lagging indicators.

- **Volume**

Volume indicators tally the information in the market and reveal the power of the bulls versus bears in the market. In short, they tell us the units of the trading instrument being sold or bought at a given time. You can find better trades by trading when the volume of bulls or bears is increasing (depending on whether you are buying or selling).

Some examples of volume indicators are Chaikin Money Flow, On-Balance-Volume, and Klinger Volume Oscillator.

Volume indicators can be lagging or leading, depending on the one being used.

- **Momentum**

Momentum indicators show the strength of a trend and whether a reversal is likely to occur. They are very useful in finding peaks and troughs. As such, they can be useful in knowing when or where to enter or exit a trade.

Some examples of momentum indicators are the Average Directional Index (ADX), Relative Strength Index (RSI), and the Stochastic.

These indicators are leading.

- **Volatility**

Volatility indicators show us the rate of price changes in the market at a specific time. Volatility is important since we need the markets to move so we can ride trends and make some profits. A higher volatility means the prices are moving fast, so the market is trending well.

Some examples of volatility indicators include Bollinger Bands and Average True Range.

Volatility indicators are lagging indicators.

POPULAR CHART INDICATORS

Below, we shall look at one example of an indicator from each of the four categories and how they can be used in day trading.

First, you need to have the chart of the trading instrument that you need to analyze open then follow the following steps:

- In your MT5, click on the "View" menu at the top of the program

- Next, click on "Navigator." A panel will open to the left side. It contains folders that have the indicators inside.

- From here, you need to choose the type of indicator that you want to apply. If it is a trend indicator, click on the (+) sign next to the "Trend Folder" in the panel. It will open a list of trend indicators.

- To add any of the trend indicators to your active chart, click and drag it into the chart, then press "okay." The indicator will appear in your chart.

- To remove an indicator from the chart, right-click inside the open window, click on the "indicator list," then click on the indicator that you want to remove and press "delete."

You will do the same when attaching or removing the other indicators. Just look inside the relevant folders, then drag the indicators into the chart you want to analyze.

The Moving Average (Trend)

Attach the moving average to your chart. It will appear as a line.

The moving average, popularly known as the MA, is the most common indicator used in trading. It is very useful in that it reveals price action by filtering out the noise from the market through smoothing. As you can see from your chart, the MA sometimes goes up, down, or stays in a straight line.

MAs use a parameter known as "periods" in displaying the price action. The period refers to the number of days that the indicator will look into the past and then smooth the closing prices to give you a line that shows us the market direction. You can edit the period to be used by going to indicator list > moving average, then under "Parameters," edit the number of days that you need under "Period." When you click "OK," the moving average will be displayed.

When the period is too low, the MA will be very sensitive to price and will show a line that follows almost every move of the market. If the period is increased, the displayed MA smoothens and shows the average direction of the market. The most common periods used in MAs are 21, 50, 120, and 200.

Let us attach a 21 and 50-period MA to our charts and see how they look.

21 and 50-period moving averages

INTERPRETING MAS

From the image above, you can see that the 21-period MA reacts more to price than the 50-period MA. To read the trend, we look at the position of the market in relation to the MA's position. If the price is above the MA, then we have an uptrend. When the price is below the MA, then we have a downtrend. You can use any period of your choice alongside the previous tools that we learned.

Have you realized what happens when the two MAs cross? Look again! On the left side of the above image, you can see that when the 21 MA crossed above the 50 MA, the price went up. Similarly, when the 21 crossed below the 50 on the right side, we had a smooth downtrend movement. So, you use single MAs or MA crossovers to confirm candlestick patterns or support and resistance signals.

Bollinger Bands (Volatility)

Remove the MAs from your chart and attach the Bollinger Bands (BB). You will find it under the "Examples" folder in the Navigator window.

The BB is yet another favorite indicator used by traders. It consists of a moving average placed between two lines on either side. The two outer lines are known as the bands. Bollinger Bands are used in revealing the volatility in the market as well as the trend and future areas of support and resistance. As you can tell, it is an all-around system. However, you should never use it as the sole guide in your trading; remember that price action remains the best lead.

Here is a BB attached to a chart:

The Bollinger Bands indicator

Interpreting Bollinger Bands

The two outer bands show the volatility in the market. When they come close together, it means there is minimal volatility (price movement). You can see that even the candles formed in such areas are small. On the other hand, when the bands expand and move away from each other, it means there is a lot of volatility in the market.

This indicator has many interesting uses. It can also be used in trading-ranging markets. If you have already spotted a ranging market using our previous tools, attach the bands to your chart. You can look at what we call the "Bollinger Bounce" to trade a stagnant market. During these periods, the price will tend to touch any of the outer bands and then return to the MA in the middle. As such, you can confirm your trades using this indicator.

The other way you can trade using BBs is to wait for breakouts when the market is trending. If the price breaks out of the upper bands, there are chances that an uptrend will continue. Similarly, if the price breaks out of the lower band, then expect a downtrend. A "break" means that the body of a candlestick is closed outside any of the bands. Do not consider the wicks. I will never get tired of reminding you to only use indicators as confirmations of potential trade opportunities that you have spotted using candlestick formations and support and resistance zones.

Note: You can tweak the parameters of the BB to suit your trading style. Go to "Indicator List" > "BB"> "Inputs" and play around with the numbers.

Relative Strength Index (Momentum)

Our third chart indicator is known as the Relative Strength Index, RSI. It appears on a different window below the chart of the instrument being traded. The RSI is simply a line that oscillates between two levels (0 and 100). There are two more levels between the 0 and 100 marked as 70 and 30. These are the ones that we shall pay more attention to.

Let us see how the RSI looks in the charts.

The RSI indicator

INTERPRETING THE RSI

The RSI tries to show us when the market is overbought or oversold so we can expect reversals. When the blue line touches the upper (70) mark, the market is said to be overbought. In short, the bulls have utilized all their buying power so they might not push the market any higher. When the line touches the lower mark (30), the market is said to be oversold and might reverse soon. Here, the bears have utilized much of their selling power, so the market might not sink any further.

Due to this predictive power, the RSI is used in finding tops and bottoms. You can see from the above image that when the price touched the overbought line, it would fall later. Similarly, when it touched the oversold line, the price would rise in the future.

On-Balance Volume (Volume)

Our final chart indicator is known as the On-Balance Volume, OBV. As the name suggests, it is a volume indicator and will reveal whether the bulls or bears are in charge of a market. Reading the OBV is very simple since all you need to do is to look at the sharp tops and bottoms that it forms. Next, you should draw a line to connect only the very dominant tops and bottoms. Look at the image below.

The OBV indicator

Interpreting the OBV

When observing the tops and bottoms, identify where they are forming higher Highs and lower Lows or lower Highs and lower Lows. Next, use the "Draw Trendline" tool found at the top-left side of your MT5 to join these important points.

If the resulting trendline is sloping up, then there is a more bullish volume. In this case, you should only look for buy trades. If the trendline is sloping downward, then there is more bearish volume, so you should only look for sell trades.

SUMMARY

Your trading arsenal is growing!

Indicators are very useful tools when they are used appropriately. Unfortunately, some trainers and marketers mislead potential traders that there are magical indicators that can be used as standalone tools to spot accurate trades. I almost fell into that trap when I was starting out back in the day. Believe it or not, I spent over two years searching for the best indicator to make me a profitable trader, but I never came across even one!

In the end, I had to embrace the fact that I had always been told that price action is the best indicator of trading.

The four indicators that we have discussed here are drawn from each of the four categories. Therefore, if you included all of them in your chart, each of them would give you different information. If you add the information that they show you to the support and resistance zones, as well as candlesticks strategies, the trades that you spot will most likely be profitable.

Finally, you need to understand that there are more volume, momentum, trend, and volatility indicators that you can use. The four indicators that we used in this chapter are meant to show you how different indicators can show different market information. I also chose the four specifically because they are simple yet very efficient if you use them properly. In short, you can research more indicators and practice using them in your charts. The only warning that I would give is that indicators should never replace your price action skills!

In the following chapters, we shall discuss some of the best day trading strategies that you can use to make a living. They will combine price action, a few indicators, and, of course, new interesting trading skills.

CHAPTER 11
ELLIOT WAVES

In the early 1920s, when stock trading was still an emerging profession, a seasoned stock trader named Ralph Elliot made a wonderful discovery that changed the entire trading industry. After analyzing the market for over 70 years, he discovered that the markets do not move randomly but follow some repetitive cycles. He named these cycles "waves." According to Elliot, the upward and downward movements of the markets were based on the collective psychology of the traders, and by understanding this, predicting the markets would be easy.

FRACTALS

To explain the wave theory, Elliot used fractals to explain the market. Fractals are objects or elements that can be split into parts, and the smaller resulting parts will be similar to the original object. For instance, if you split a snowflake, it will produce smaller snowflakes that will be similar to the larger one. Similarly, when a huge cloud breaks up, the smaller clouds that are born bear the same shape and color as the parent cloud.

According to Elliot, the markets also follow the same principle. Whenever there is an uptrend, there will be smaller uptrends inside the main trend. The same is true during a downtrend. Therefore, by identifying fractals, we can predict the direction of the market and trade according to the main trend.

THE 5-3 WAVE PATTERN

This concept identified by Elliot came to be known as the "Elliot Wave Theory." It shows that when a market is trending, it follows something called the 5-3 wave pattern. In the pattern, there are two waves.

The first part of the pattern is made up of 5 waves that are known as the Impulse Waves. They move along the main trend.

The second part of the pattern is made up of 3 waves that are known as Corrective Waves. These waves move against the main trend.

Below is an image for a better understanding of this concept:

Elliot waves showing an uptrend and downtrend

In the image above, the wave on the left shows an uptrend. As you can see, there are 3 smaller waves that make up the larger upward movement. Waves 1, 3, and 5 move upward (impulse), while 2 and 4 oppose the main trend (corrective). Generally, the 5 waves work together to create an uptrend.

The image on the right shows a downtrend. Just like the one on the left, there are 3 impulse waves that follow the main downtrend and 2 corrective waves that oppose the main trend. Collectively, they create a downtrend.

Before we head over to the charts to try and identify the Elliot waves, here are the five cardinal rules used in identifying and validating the 5 waves:

- **Wave 1:** The first impulse wave is the beginning of a new trend. It happens when the traders in the market feel that the instrument is ready for buying or selling.

- **Wave 2:** After a small upward or downward movement, the traders who had started wave 1 might think the instrument is overvalued, so many will take profits. When this happens, the market will go up or down a little and form a short corrective wave. However, the new high or low that is formed can never be equal to the starting point of wave 1.

- **Wave 3:** When the new high or low is formed in wave 2 and fails to go past the starting point of wave 1, attentive traders realize that the instrument has established a new trend so they will place trades in huge numbers. This results in the formation of a very long wave 3. For this wave to be valid, it must move past the high or low formed by the end of wave 1. Wave 3 is usually the strongest and longest impulsive wave.

- **Wave 4:** After wave 3 has been active for some time, it becomes oversold or overbought (you can use an indicator to spot this). The reaction of most traders is to take the profits that wave 3 gave them before the market starts reversing. When they close their trades, the market reverses for a very short distance. However, trend traders know that the trend will continue, so they do not close their trades. This leads to the formation of a very short corrective wave 4 before the trend continues. Wave 4 is usually shorter than wave 2, but it should be higher than wave 2's ending point.

- **Wave 5:** Immediately wave 4 is completed; the final move of the trend starts forming. This is the wave where most of the traders who know how to study the market will place their trades. Wave 5 is usually driven by uncontrollable excitement known as hysteria. At times, impulse wave 5 will be very strong that it might be longer than wave 3. Since it is the last move in the trend, it tends to happen very fast. This is the time when most traders make or lose money.

- **The ABC wave:** At the end of wave 5, you might wonder what happens to the market. What happens is that if wave 5 was correctly identified, the overall trend starts reversing. In short, the 5-wave trend is corrected by a 3-wave countertrend formation.

The ABC wave that comes after wave 5 is also used in hunting for moves. In our case, though, we are going to stop at wave 5 since the moves that occur from the first wave to the last one are enough for day trading. In addition, the ABC wave can be a little confusing. For now, let us head over to the charts and try to identify some Elliot waves.

Below is an excellent Elliot wave in an uptrend.

Below is an excellent Elliot wave during a downtrend.

At this level, you have become an intermediate trader. Therefore, the above charts with Elliot waves should be self-explanatory. In your opinion, do the two waves in both charts adhere to the 5 rules of the Elliot wave theory? Second, are you able to spot the areas where you would have plotted your support and resistance zones? Are there any candlestick patterns in the turning points of the waves?

TRADING WITH ELLIOT WAVES

Day trading is interesting, as you can tell from the lessons that you have received so far, right? This guide has simplified the best concepts of trading so that you understand and apply them without struggling. The best thing about the training that you are getting is that it uses price action and very basic tools to turn you into a professional day trader.

Now that you understand how the Elliot wave theory works, it is time to see how it can be used in trading using the concepts that you have acquired so far.

In the following sections, we shall use the two above charts with Elliot waves to see if all the concepts created confluence and gave us winning trades.

Elliot Waves, Candlesticks, and Support & Resistance

A quick reminder here: when you open a new chart, the first thing that you should do is to identify and mark out the main areas of support and resistance. This is the first step in revealing the trend direction as well as where to look for potential trading signals. Refer back to the support and resistance chapter until you are able to identify these critical zones easily.

Now, our bullish chart with candlestick patterns and support and resistance included:

DISCUSSION

Point 1 is our starting area. You can see from the left that we had a downtrend that was approaching the strong area of support below the market. Let us assume that we had been watching the price as it came to touch our support.

Upon hitting the support, you can see that the candles began decreasing in size, and long wicks were formed. These are signs of the price being rejected (bulls pushing the bears away, so they cannot take the market any lower). This is the first event that would have caught our attention. We can see that price tried to go higher, formed a Higher-High, then fell back to support where it faced more rejection and formed a Higher-Low. At this point, we had confirmed that wave 1 and wave 2 formations were in progress.

As the price bounced off the support for the second time, we would have been waiting for wave 2 to close, so we could enter the trade in the direction of the new trend (upward). A few candles later, we had a perfect three bullish soldiers pattern formed, and that confirmed that wave 2 was complete. After the last candle of the pattern closed, we would have entered the trade at the opening of the next candle, which was the start of wave 3.

Our stop-loss would go below the support level that gave us the entry while the take-profit would go in or near the next resistance zone. We would expect wave 3 to form near the next resistance area, which it did! We call this area, Take-Profit Level 1. This is because, as per the Elliot wave theory, a trend is not complete until it forms wave 5. As such, we would wait for wave 4 to pull back a little (correct). To identify the potential distance that the wave would correct, we look at the starting point of wave 2. Wave 3 should not reach that point. Second, we look to the left of the chart and identify a small support zone. That is where wave 4 is likely to end, and wave 5 would start.

In the image above, you can see that wave 4 obeyed

all these rules. It neither broke past the high of wave 1 nor the small area of support below it. In addition, it formed a bullish engulfing pattern, and wave 5 was confirmed. We could also have opened another buy here and placed our take-profit above the high of wave 3 and close to the next resistance zone. This would be our Take-Profit Level 3. Our stop-loss would be placed below the small support zone where wave 4 ended, and wave 5 began.

Assuming that we had taken both of these trades, we would have won in both. Do you see how the price took off and never went near our stop-loss levels?

Dear trader, this is how you read the market like an open book.

Next, we are going to dissect the bearish Elliot wave movement using candlestick patterns as well as support and resistance.

DISCUSSION

Did you try to interpret this chart on your own?

As usual, we need to identify an existing trend that is headed toward a zone of support or resistance. In the above chart, we had an uptrend that had formed after bouncing off a support level. Let us assume that we had been watching the price rise. At the top of the chart, we had a strong resistance zone judging from the left side.

So, when the price touched the resistance zone, we see that it formed a bearish engulfing pattern. It went back up and formed some short candles, with the longer wicks appearing on the upper sides before another engulfing pattern was formed. Can you spot it? At this point, we do not have any wave 1 in sight. Price sank a little, and we would have thought that it had left without us. However, it reached a small support zone and bounced back into the resistance zone. We can see this from the rejection of the candles and the formation of a bullish engulfing pattern.

At this point, we have a clear impulse wave 1. The current wave would be corrective wave 2. We would watch to see if it would go higher than the start of wave 1, which it failed to do! Instead, the price faced massive rejection and later formed a huge bearish engulfing pattern. This is where we would mark the end of wave 2 and the beginning of the juicy wave 3. Our sell trade would be opened at the close of the last candle forming the bearish engulfing pattern.

As always, our protective stop-loss goes above the resistance level that gave us the trade. We are going to place our Take-Profit Level 1 in or near the next strong support area. As you can see, the price fell without going back to the stop-loss, and it would have hit our take-profit level very easily. At this level, we would have expected wave 3 to end and wave 4 to start the corrective movement.

Do you see how the market went into the support zone and looked like it had broken it without bouncing up? This is normal, and it only shows that the bears were very powerful. Again, we had a longer wave 3. Can you spot the small candles that started forming below the support area? Do you see that bullish engulfing pattern? The market rose again and went past our support. This was a clear wave 4 in progress. It went up until it met a small resistance zone, formed a huge wick that was followed by a clear bearish engulfing pattern.

This would mark the end of wave 4 and the start of wave 5. We would enter a second trade here (if we wanted) and placed our stop-loss slightly above the small resistance level where wave 4 ended. Our Take-Profit Level 2 would go below the point where wave 3 ended; that is in or near the next support level.

Just like our first trade, the second one would have also given us some easy, handsome profits that were almost risk-free.

Elliot Waves and Indicators

The power of Elliot waves is endless. I believe that you can now identify them easily using their anatomy with the aid of trends, as well as support and resistance. We are now going to see how indicators can add to the accuracy of the Elliot waves using the same charts that we used above.

I will place three of the indicators that we looked at in the previous chapter in the same chart, so we can see what each one of them will be telling us. You can add the Bollinger Bands, RSI, and OBV indicators to your charts. I have not said the Moving Average because the BB already has a moving average in it.

A chart with the three indicators, support, and resistance zones, as well as our Elliot Wave, should look like this:

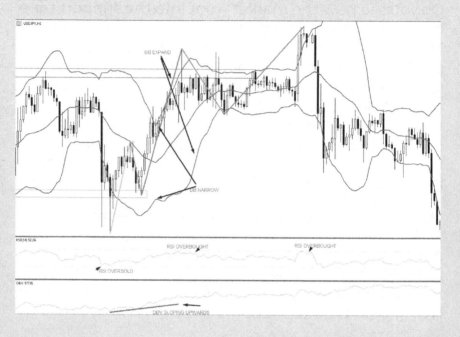

DISCUSSION

Sorry about the confusing chart above. The biggest reason that we discourage the use of too many indicators is that they can be confusing and misleading, and they also make the charts messy. However, pardon me for today because I had to bundle all of them into the charts, so we can discuss them all at once. Remember that you will have to choose the ones that you find most useful for your trading.

BOLLINGER BANDS

The BB has a Moving Average in the middle. I have set mine to period 21 so that it can react faster to the price and confirm my entries. We are day traders, so MAs with very low sensitivity might lead to missing trade opportunities. Look at where wave 1 ended and wave 2 began. Did the price break above the MA? No! Therefore, we had no permission to buy. The price was rejected, and it fell back to the support, and wave 2 ended as wave 3 began. This time, the price broke past the MA since a candle closed above it. As such, we would have taken our buy entry here.

At the same time, when the price was struggling to break the 21 MA, the bands of the BB were close together. However, when the MA was broken, the bands expanded. This is yet another confirmation since volatility had increased.

Finally, on the BB, do you see where the market touches the outer bands in the presence of our support and resistance zones? It is clear that those areas are very strong, and the market behaves as we would expect. You can see that it is at those points that the Elliot waves change from the impulse to corrective waves and vice-versa.

RSI

The RSI is quite straightforward. Look at where wave 1 began. A few candles before, the RSI had touched the oversold (30) level. It told us to expect a new trend. Magically, the trend happened after some candles! However, we did not follow the RSI blindly; we waited for confirmation from candle patterns and the bounce from the support area.

Look at where wave 3 ended. The RSI was clearly in the overbought (70) level while coinciding with a resistance zone. As such, we had been expecting the market to slow down and reverse to form wave 4. Just like magic, the market pulled back, and we had our wave 4 formed! The next time that the RSI touched the overbought level, wave 5 had formed, and we would have taken our profits there.

OBV

The OBV is also very simple yet very powerful. You can see that it began forming Higher-Highs and Higher-Lows when the price was at our support level and when the previous downtrend had ended. Therefore, in this area, we had the confluence from all our indicators that a new trend had started. With this information in mind, you would not find yourself trying to sell, as that would be opposing the trend. Also, the fact that the OBV told us about a new trend means that we caught the Elliot wave in its early stages of formation. As you can see from the indicator, the entire move was an uptrend as no Lower-Lows or Lower-Highs were formed.

SUMMARY

Pat yourself on the back if this is how you would have had interpreted the above chart. You are now one of the best traders of your time just from the few lessons that you have received. I hope that you now believe that trading is not easy, but it can be made simple. To the untrained eye, all the concepts that you have studied would appear like Greek alphabets. However, to you, the newest trader on the block, you understand each and every one of them, courtesy of this guide. Now, all you need to do is to take your time and apply these concepts in live trading using your demo account. Consistent practice is the surest way to grasp and internalize your training. Persevere for now because soon, you will be able to spot these winning opportunities with utmost ease and precision.

Let us conclude this chapter by shouting together that, *"Elliot Waves are real!"*

CHAPTER 12
THE ABCD PATTERN

The ABCD trading pattern is a relative of the Elliot Waves in the sense that it is based on the fact that the market moves in an organized manner. In addition, it is one of the most profitable day trading strategies that you can find out there. Since the pattern is based on pure price action and follows market structure, it is a powerful leading indicator.

STRUCTURE

The pattern uses impulse and corrective waves to predict the future of the market. The points named A, B, C, and D represent significant highs and lows in the market. When points A and B are joined, they form a wave known as a "leg." As such, the pattern is made up of legs AB, BC, and CD, where AB and CD are impulse waves, and BC is a corrective wave. AB and CD should be parallel to each other. We predict the future of the market by placing trades at the end of leg CD and in the direction of BC.

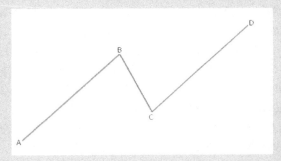

- Leg AB is equal to Leg CD in the "classic ABCD" pattern.

- Leg CD can extend by 127.2% or 161.8% in the "ABCD extension" pattern (more of the percentages later).

- The time it takes to form AB is the same it should take to form CD in the "Classic ABCD" pattern.

- Leg BC is the corrective wave and gives the direction of reversal after the completion of the leg CD.

Before we go any further into this pattern, we need to discuss an important tool that should be used alongside the pattern for better analysis. It is called the Fibonacci sequence tool.

THE FIBONACCI SEQUENCE

The Fibonacci sequence is yet another important concept used in market analysis. It is very important in identifying the potential support and resistance areas, as well as the future movement of the market. It utilizes a little bit of mathematics to explain that everything in nature has a pattern known as the golden ratio that can be identified and used to explain things. For instance, the golden ratio can be used to count the number of veins in a leaf or the bones in a human being. We will not go too much into the mathematical derivations, as they are not very important to our lesson.

Retracement Levels

The Fibonacci uses what we call retracement and extension levels to analyze the market. Retracement levels are the points in the market where a trend will pull back (correct) from the main trend before resuming the overall direction. In short, retracement levels can tell us how far waves 2 and 4 in the Elliot wave will go with more accuracy. In the ABCD pattern, these levels will tell us how far leg BC will move in proportion to leg AB.

The Fibonacci retracement levels are denoted as 0.236 (23.6%), 0.382 (38.2%), 0.500 (50%), and 0.764 (76.4%). You will understand them better when we draw them in the charts.

Extension Levels

On the other hand, extension levels tell us how far the market will move in relation to a previous leg in the past. In the ABCD pattern, for example, we can predict how far led CD will move in relation to leg AB. As we stated in the structure of the ABCD pattern, in some cases, leg CD can be 127.2% or 161.8% longer than leg AB. The Fibonacci tool will help to identify these extensions.

The Fibonacci extension levels are 0 (0%), 0.382 (38.2%), 0.618 (61.8%), 1.000 (100%), 1.382 (138.2%), and 1.618 (161.8%).

Using the Fibonacci Tool

To use the Fibonacci tool, you first need to identify some swing highs and swing lows in the market. A swing high is a point in the market that has at least 2 Lower-Highs on either side. In short, there should be a dominant candle and two or more lower-highs on its right and left sides. A swing low is the opposite of a swing high. It is a candlestick that has 2 higher-lows on either side.

To plot the Fibonacci levels, you use the Fibonacci Retracement tool found on the top-right side of your MT5 platform. It looks like this:

Draw Fibonacci retracement

Plotting Retracement Levels

Remember that a retracement level means the points where the price might reverse (correct) from the main trend before resuming the general trend.

In an uptrend, you need to identify the most recent swing high and the most recent swing low. Choose the Fibonacci tool, click it, drag it from the swing high up to the swing low, and then release it. It will draw the retracement levels for you like below:

As you can see, after drawing the Fibonacci retracements in the uptrend market, the price pulled back and reached the 61.8% level, where it found support and went back to the main trend.

To plot the retracements during a downtrend, you need to use the Fibonacci tool and click on the most recent swing low and drag it up to the most recent swing high. Your chart will look like this:

From the image, you can see how the downtrend reversed up to the 38.2% and 23.6% levels before it resumed its initial main direction. Clearly, Fibonacci levels can be used as support and resistance points.

Plotting Extension Levels

Fibonacci extension levels are plotted the same as the retracement levels. However, you need to tweak your tool a little by manually adding the extension levels that you want. To do so, attach the tool to your desired chat. Then double-click on the diagonal line in the tool to highlight it. Some three small squares will appear on the line. Next, right-click on any of the dots then go to "Properties" > "Levels." Find the level described as "100."

Now, you need to edit the number below 100. Double-click inside the first box below the 100, edit it to 138.2 and then change the level on the left side of it to 1.382. Click and edit the box below the 138.2, and edit it to 161.8. Also, edit the level to its right to 1.618. You can add or remove levels as desired. Click "OK," and the new levels will show up in your charts.

The extension levels are used in taking profits since they show the area where the market might move before slowing down or reversing. Here is a chart showing an extension level in a downtrend:

In the above image, you can see how the price went down after the retracement move. If a trader had placed their take-profit levels at either the 138.2 or 161.8% levels, they would have made their profits. You can also see how the two extension levels held the price for some time. Please note that these lines were plotted before the price had formed, yet the market respected them when it got to them. That is the magic of the Fibonacci tool!

Now, let us go back to the ABCD Pattern, and see how it is combined with the Fibonacci tool for the best results.

CLASSIC ABCD PATTERN

The classic bullish ABCD pattern looks like the following image:

a) Classic bearish ABCD   b) Classic bullish ABCD

In the above images:

- The length of AB is equal to the length of the leg CD

- The time it takes to form AB is the same it takes to form CD

- Point C should not go near point A. Similarly, point D should not be near point C. In short, you should have clear swing points indicating a good trend.

- The leg BC should retrace to 127.2% or 161.8% of BC. To plot this, since we have an uptrend, the Fibonacci would be drawn from point B (swing high) up to point A (swing low). Then as the market unfolded, it would bounce off C (retracement level) and continue to create leg CD. Once the trader is sure that the classic ABCD has been completed, they can enter a sell trade at point D (reversal into a downtrend).

EXTENDED ABCD PATTERN

An extended ABCD pattern is different from the classic ABCD pattern in that the leg CD can be longer than leg AB by between 127.2% and 161.8%. Also, the time that it takes to form CD can extend by the same percentages. This pattern should look something like this:

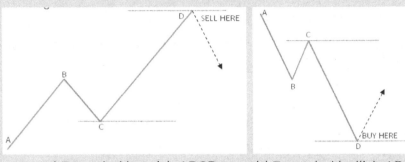

a) Extended bearish ABCD   b) Extended bullish ABCD

Here are two examples of the ABCD pattern in the charts.

Extended bearish ABCD pattern

Classic bullish ABCD pattern

Trading with the ABCD Pattern

You can add some of the other tools like support & resistance to your ABCD pattern trading style to improve the accuracy of the turning points. The stronger a zone is, the more likely that your leg is accurate. Fibonacci levels also work well when combined with support & resistance zones. Confluence at turning points or entry points can be increased by utilizing the knowledge of candlestick formations or a few indicators. However, be careful not to have too many tools in your charts as this can lead to analysis paralysis.

You must always keep in mind that no trading strategy is foolproof. You might have the best analysis and find the most promising trade signals, but still, the market might ignore and oppose you. Therefore, to be safe from excess losses, make sure to always have a protective stop-loss order immediately after you place a trade. The ABCD pattern makes stop-loss placement very easy. You need to identify a zone below or above point D and place it there. The First Take-Profit Level can be placed at the level of C. You can have a Second Take-Profit Level at point A or where your Fibonacci extension level coincides with strong support or resistance level.

SUMMARY

How did you find this lesson? Was it as engaging and informative as I felt when it was first taught to me? I hope that you found it that way.

As always, I will emphasize two things: first, you have the freedom to choose which tools work for you. My objective here was to show you the best tools for day trading so that you can choose one or two or all of them! Second, put in as much practice time as you can with these strategies. Some of them, like the Elliot Waves and the ABCD pattern, require a lot of time to form. Therefore, exercise patience and do not be disappointed if a pattern fails, or it takes too long to give you a signal. Eventually, you will start seeing the importance of only taking the best trade signals and leaving the rest.

CHAPTER 13
RISK MANAGEMENT

N ow that you are a qualified trader, you will come across people who will tell you that day trading is gambling. I used to get angry or disappointed when I was told the same. After some thoughtful consideration, I realized that they were right and wrong at the same time. They were right because the trading industry benefits the big players more than the retail speculators. Just like in all sorts of gambling, the casinos always win. The part of them being wrong is that it depends on the approaches that individual traders apply when fighting with the big boys, and this is where the aspect of risk management comes in.

Risk management is simply the aspect of controlling risks and ensuring that you have the edge over the market. Concisely, you need to install measures that will not only improve your winning but also ensure that your losses are insignificant. Remember that in the trading industry, losses are part and parcel of the process. However, your losses must be kept at a minimum so that in the long run, your portfolio will always be in profits. In my many years at trading, I have come to conclude that many traders who end up losing and quitting are those who ignore risk management.

Below are some of the ways that I have learned over the years that can help you in managing your risks and always being on the winning side.

FOLLOW THE TREND

I have repeated this concept more than enough times within the book. Use your learned knowledge of identifying market swing highs and lows to know where the trend is heading. Build more confluence on matters of market direction by using indicators like the Moving Average or the OBV. Opposing the overall trend is suicidal.

USE A STOP-LOSS

A stop-loss controls how much you are willing to risk for each trade. First of all, never trade without a stop-loss! Second, know where to place the stop-loss so that it is neither too close nor too far from your entry. A small stop-loss distance might be hit too soon, while a huge stop-loss distance can lead to excess losses.

USE PROPER RISK TO REWARD

The risk to reward ratio is the best risk management approach to keep you in profits. It makes use of the stop-loss and take-profit orders collectively. The idea of this approach is to place your take-profit levels at least two times further than the stop-loss. In short, if your stop-loss distance is 20 pips, place your take-profit level at least 40 pips away.

You should consider the risk to reward ratio before entering any trade. Look at your tools of analysis such as support & resistance, Fibonacci, ABCD legs, and Elliot Waves to see which trades have a better risk to reward potential. If a trade has a 1:1 ratio (equal stop-loss and take-profit distance), consider ignoring it. Take only the trades that have a 1:2 or 1:3 risk to reward ratio only. Are you wondering why?

The concept is simple: if you place a 1:3 trade and it wins, it would take three losing trades (stop-loss is hit) to lose all the profit that you made. As such, even if you won only 3 out of every 5 trades that you made, you would still be in profit.

USE CORRECT POSITION SIZING

Position sizing refers to how much of your capital you will risk at a go. In general, we always advise that each trade should not risk more than 2% of your trading capital. This is to say that if you have $200 in your trading account, your stop-loss should not risk more than $4. It would take 50 losses to lose all your $200. Do you get it?

Now, assume that you risked $20 per trade. You would only have to lose ten times, and your account would be wiped clean. Therefore, keep the position size very small.

USE MINIMAL LEVERAGE

Leverage is known as the double-edged sword in online trading since it can bring a trade a lot of profit in a short time or take away as much money in a similar duration. Leverage allows you to borrow more money from your broker and place more or bigger trades. To be safe, use minimal leverage so that your risk is insignificant. When you have a leverage of 1,000, it means that for every dollar that you have, the broker can let you borrow 1,000 times more money. If you place a trade with such high leverage, it will take a few seconds before your account got wiped. Use minimal leverage that will allow you to risk less than 2% of your trading capital per trade.

AVOID OVERTRADING

Trading is addictive; do not say you were never warned! Loving your job is an awesome feeling, but when it becomes addictive, then there is a problem. Try to control your trading time so that you are not always on the charts. Just like a typical job, fix the best time to be trading. Conduct a little research on the market that you are going to be trading and find out the best time to trade. In most cases, the best trading occurs when the majority of traders are active since there are enough volatility and volume for good trends to occur. Lastly, once you meet your daily trading targets, end your trading day and wait for another day.

CONTROL YOUR EMOTIONS

The last and very important risk management trick is to take full charge of your emotions. The markets are controlled by human psychology; as such, you can gain an advantage in your trading by understanding how the markets work. This book has taught you enough of that. At a personal level, there are three types of emotions that you must keep in check for you to be successful at day trading:

- **Fear**

We can agree on the fact that trading is a risky career since it involves putting money on the line. Therefore, at some point in your trading, especially when you first start trading with a real account, you might be afraid of placing trades. This is normal, but you should not allow it to control your trading activity since it can lead to missed trading opportunities.

The reason you have been taught several of the best trading strategies in existence is for you to be able to place your trades with confidence. If you conduct accurate analysis and implement the right risk management principles, then you should have nothing to worry about your trades.

- **Overconfidence**

You should also manage the level of confidence that you have. Too much confidence might make you forget that the market is ruthless and does not obey anyone. When you forget the rules, you might end up taking premature signals, relying on automated systems, overriding proper position sizing, and generally exposing yourself to more risks.

Be confident, but keep the protective rules at your fingertips.

- **Greed**

Once you start raking in dollars, which I assure you that you will, do not be greedy. Overconfidence can lead to greed. You might find yourself risking too much of your account, placing a lot of trades, overtrading, and increasing your leverage in pursuit of more dollars. This might work for a short time, but eventually, a single silly mistake will place you on the bad side of the market, and that might leave you with deep psychological wounds and an empty wallet. Who wants that?

Risk management is as important to your trading as the strategy. You might have the best strategy in the world, but without proper risk management, you will end up with losses. Every profession in the world has its own rules that govern the safety and experience of the workers. Online trading is no different; you must utilize risk management. Put in as many of these concepts as you can, and you will find that trading is very easy. In addition, risk management cuts off the gambling aspect of trading.

CHAPTER 14
CREATING YOUR TRADING PLAN

Our final chapter is dedicated to helping you to wrap everything up in a single package and boost your organization as a day trader. A serious trader needs a trading plan. This is more of a personal trading constitution that defines every aspect of your trading life. It defines why you are a trader and how you should trade at all times. The trading plan acts as a checklist that must be fulfilled before pressing the buy or sell button.

There is no definite template for a trading plan because each trader records what they feel is helpful to the trading. However, this does not make the trading plan optional; it is a must! In addition, it must be written down and accorded the respect that a constitution demands.

Here are some of the elements to include in a trading plan.

WHY ARE YOU A TRADER?

The first component in your trading plan should be about yourself. You need to have clear motivation as to why you want to be a trader. Is it financial freedom? Do you love freelancing? Do bosses scare you? Whatever your motivation might be, list it down, as it will help to keep you going even during tough times.

WHAT WILL YOU BE TRADING?

You must be very specific on the market and financial instruments that you will be trading. If you decide to trade stocks, binary options, futures, cryptocurrency, or forex, list it down. Narrow your definition further and list the specific instruments that you will be trading within your chosen market. For example, if you will be trading cryptocurrency, will you go for Bitcoin or Ethereum?

HOW WILL YOU EVALUATE YOURSELF?

Every business needs to evaluate its performance and know whether it is making profits or losses. Similarly, you need to come up with some ways to tell whether you are growing or not. You can decide to conduct your evaluation after a number of trades or after certain durations.

DEFINE YOUR TRADING STRATEGY

You should list all the components in your trading strategy and ensure that you adhere to them before executing any trades. List the way that you will be conducting your analysis from the analysis stage to the time you enter a trade. If you use indicators, define them, and explain how you will use them.

Do not forget to include stop-loss and take-profits.

WHEN WILL YOU TRADE?

A trader must be orderly enough to know when they will be at their trading desk or not. If you decide to work in the morning or when specific markets are opening, then list that in your trading plan. Make sure that you are not on the charts at a time when the plan says that you should be elsewhere.

HOW MUCH WILL YOU INVEST?

By the time you decide to deposit money with a broker so you can go live, you should have known how much money you can afford to use in trading. Initially, only invest what you can afford to lose without losing your mind. You can grow your capital as your experience expands.

Position sizing should also come here. You must decide how much money to risk per trade. Make sure you adhere to the money management rules that you come up with, no matter how appealing a trading setup looks.

WHO WILL BE YOUR BROKER?

The choice of broker that you go for is crucial to your trading success. Conduct proper research on the best broker to work with. Some qualities of a good broker include:

- They are regulated by a relevant monetary body.

- They offer all the instruments that you need to trade.

- They are cheap in terms of commissions and other charges.

- They are reputable in all aspects.

- They are accessible any time you need them.

WHAT ARE YOUR STRENGTHS AND WEAKNESSES?

Finally, you must evaluate yourself and see which of your traits make you a better trader and which ones limit your potential. Identifying your strengths will keep you motivated, and you will pay more attention to your stronger side. On the other hand, identifying your weaknesses will allow you to know what needs some improvement. You will become a better trader as you work on more of your limitations.

These are just some of the elements that you can include in your trading plan. You can add more as you please, as long as they add value to your trading career. The most important thing, however, is that you follow the rules in your constitution to the end. If you only compose it and stop at that, it will be as good as seeing a good trade setup and letting it go. One day, when you are a successful trader, you will look back at this chapter and be proud that you began creating your trading plan the very moment you realized that this is the last page in your book :)

CONCLUSION

Thank you for making it through the end of *Day Trading*. Let us hope it was engaging and informative while providing you with all the know-how that you need to achieve success in your day trading goals.

This book was composed in the best way to ensure you enjoyed studying online trading, which many people find too complicated. It brought together many years of experience and condensed the most useful knowledge to make anyone successful in trading the markets. We might say a lot, but the most important thing is that you end up a profitable trader without suffering as most traders do.

The next step is to start practicing all these concepts. Trading is a practical profession, and your success is highly determined by how much experience you have garnered. Therefore, put all the lessons in the book to practice in your MT5. You will internalize them and find that using them to spot winning trades is not only easy but also enjoyable. As you practice some more, you will settle on the best ones to be used in your daily trading life.

Finally, if you found this book useful in any way, I would appreciate it if you could recommend it to other people, as well as give it a review on Amazon. Thank you in advance for your consideration.

I wish you the very best as you start your successful day trading career. Thanks again!

TAKE YOUR GIFT

As a way of saying thanks for your purchase,
I'm offering an **EXTRA BONUS**:

 Glossary of useful terms linked to markets
in financial instruments
Excel portfolio management models
Book (PDF - full color) of this book

Scan the QR Code with your mobile phone
and request your **GIFT now!**

IF YOU LIKE THIS BOOK, HELP ME BY LEAVING A REVIEW ON AMAZON!

Scan the QR code with your mobile phone and you can immediately leave a review,

Or

1. Go to **Amazon** and click on "**My orders**"
2. Search for **this book** and click to go into details
3. Scroll down and click on   Write a customer review

Share the pages you liked the most with and post them in the reviews.

Thanks a lot! See you soon.
Mark Swing

To make sure you **don't miss any new book**, **follow my Author page on Amazon**

https://www.amazon.com/stores/Mark-Swing/author/B082MMQ6SM

Or scan this QR code with your mobile phone

I greatly appreciate your feedback and invite you to email me at markswingtrading@gmail.com with any errors or inaccuracies you encounter in the book. Your insights are invaluable to my ongoing efforts to improve the reading experience and create an even better version.

Made in United States
Orlando, FL
06 December 2024

55048457R00085